The Marquis de Sade: A Very Short Introduction

VERY SHORT INTRODUCTIONS are for anyone wanting a stimulating
and accessible way in to a new subject. They are written by experts, and have
been published in more than 25 languages worldwide.

The series began in 1995, and now represents a wide variety of topics
in history, philosophy, religion, science, and the humanities. Over the next
few years it will grow to a library of around 200 volumes – a Very Short
Introduction to everything from ancient Egypt and Indian philosophy to
conceptual art and cosmology.

Very Short Introductions available now:

Available soon:

For more information visit our web site

www.oup.co.uk/vsi/

John Phillips

THE MARQUIS DE SADE

A Very Short Introduction

OXFORD
UNIVERSITY PRESS

OXFORD
UNIVERSITY PRESS

Great Clarendon Street, Oxford OX2 6DP

Oxford University Press is a department of the University of Oxford.
It furthers the University's objective of excellence in research, scholarship,
and education by publishing worldwide in

Oxford New York

Auckland Cape Town Dar es Salaam Hong Kong Karachi
Kuala Lumpur Madrid Melbourne Mexico City Nairobi
New Delhi Shanghai Taipei Toronto

With offices in

Argentina Austria Brazil Chile Czech Republic France Greece
Guatemala Hungary Italy Japan Poland Portugal Singapore
South Korea Switzerland Thailand Turkey Ukraine Vietnam

Oxford is a registered trade mark of Oxford University Press
in the UK and in certain other countries

Published in the United States
by Oxford University Press Inc., New York

British Library Cataloguing in Publication Data
Data available

Library of Congress Cataloging in Publication Data
Data available

ISBN 0-19-280469-3

Contents

Preface

Hailed by the early 20th-century French poet Guillaume Apollinaire as 'the freest spirit who ever lived', but demonized throughout the last two hundred years as a misogynistic pornographer, and as the original proponent of sexual sadism and lustmurder, the Marquis de Sade is a creature of myth. The popular assumption that Sade was as sadistic as his monstrous fictional villains is still current today among the majority of the population who have never read a line of his work. In fact, Sade's thought, which is expressed at great length in novels, short stories, plays, critical essays, and personal correspondence, is considerably more complex than allowed by any of the simplistic labels, positive or negative, associated with this mythical reputation.

Best known as the author of four sexually violent novels that were destined to shock readers for centuries to come, Sade was, certainly, a subversive iconoclast and life-long rebel. Yet, most of his writings contained neither obscenity nor extreme violence, and many of his works of fiction are considered masterpieces of their genre. The sheer breadth and intellectual complexity of Sade's creative output encompasses the whole range of human experience, from sexuality to morality, from politics to religion, from metaphysics to aesthetics, from literature to life and death. Standing at the end of the classical era and the beginning of the modern age, Sade is, for Michel Foucault, a pivotal figure in the history of philosophy. Spanning two centuries and successive political regimes, from monarchy to empire, he is also the only French philosopher of importance to live through the French Revolution and to comment on its events as they happened. Sade was a writer of astonishing energy and remarkable courage. He was unafraid to speak his mind, and paid for this temerity with his freedom. What makes him unique, however, is a dogged determination to tell the truth about the human condition, a truth that he located, not in a soul or spirit, as most previous philosophers had done, but simply, scandalously, in the sexual body, which for him was the only reality. Were it not for his explicit use of language and complete disregard for the artificially constructed taboos of a religious morality he despised, the novelty and profundity of Sade's thought, and, above all, its fundamental modernity, would have long since secured him a place alongside the greatest authors and thinkers of the European Enlightenment.

Acknowledgements

My thanks to Pluto Press for permission to reproduce material from my *Sade: The Libertine Novels* (2001). This material has been revised and modified for inclusion in Chapters 5 and 6. In addition, Chapter 4 contains passages relating to Sade's correspondence that first appeared in my article 'Sade and Self-censorship' (*Paragraph*, March 2000, vol. 23, no. 1); and the section on *Juliette* in Chapter 6 includes a small amount of material taken from another article, '"Tout dire?": Sade and the female body' in *Murdering Marianne?: Violence, Gender and Representation in French Literature and Film*, special issue of *South Central Review*, edited by Owen Heathcote, vol. 19, no. 4–vol. 20, no. 1, Winter 2002–Spring 2003, pp. 29–43. I am grateful to both journals for permission to reproduce this material here.

Last, but not least, I should like to thank David Coward for his vigorous support and encouragement when the book was first mooted, and my editor at Oxford University Press, Marsha Filion, who made many invaluable suggestions for revision of the first draft and guided the book into print with exemplary professionalism, rare charm, and unfailing good humour.

All quotations from Sade's work are from the English-language editions listed in the Further reading, with the exception of the letters, the majority of which are taken from Richard Seaver's *The Marquis de Sade: Letters from Prison* (London: Harvill Press, 2000). Where letters are quoted from other sources, this is indicated in the References.

List of illustrations

The publisher and the author apologize for any errors or omissions in the above list. If contacted they will be pleased to rectify these at the earliest opportunity.

1. The Comte de Sade, father of Donatien Alphonse François de Sade

Chapter 1

Beyond the myth:
the real Marquis de Sade

The Marquis de Sade, or the *Misfortunes of Vice*

Donatien Alphonse François de Sade was born in 1740. His father
was the Comte de Sade, lord of lands and property in southern
Provence, inheritor of an aristocratic title with a long lineage
that can be traced back to the Middle Ages. His mother was
lady-in-waiting and poor distant relative of the Princesse de Condé.
Little Donatien was therefore born into a privileged background
and, as the only boy in the family, was doted on by a paternal
grandmother and five aunts. The most important influences in
Sade's early years, however, were his father and his paternal uncle,
the Abbé Jacques François de Sade, both of whom had a taste for
the libertine lifestyle.

Between the ages of 10 and 14, Donatien attended the Jesuit school
of Louis-le-Grand in Paris. He also had a young preceptor, the
gentle and highly intelligent Abbé Amblet, who taught him reading,
arithmetic, geography, and history, and who was the only male
member of the child's entourage who was not a libertine. At school,
the young Marquis was rigorously trained in the skills of classical
rhetoric and debating. From the Jesuits, he may also have acquired
a liking for whipping and sodomy. The Jesuits regularly whipped
the posteriors of their charges to discipline them, and it is well
known that this form of corporal punishment can arouse the victim

Libertinism

The French word *libertin* meant 'free thinker on religion' by the end of the 16th century, but during the course of the 17th century, it gradually came to designate a person leading a dissolute lifestyle. By the beginning of the 18th century, the libertine novel, which depicted the unfettered sexual activities of libertine characters, had become an important, if socially marginal, genre which frequently attacked conventional morality as well as religious orthodoxy. Sade's uncle possessed an extensive library of such works, of which *L'Ecole des filles, Dom Bougre, ou Le Portier de Chartreux*, and *Thérèse philosophe* are well-known examples. Many such novels were sexually explicit, graphically descriptive, and obscene. Libertinism and pornography thus became closely associated. By the mid-18th century, both served an increasingly political agenda, satirizing a corrupt and unpopular church, aristocracy, and monarchy. Sade's own contribution to this tradition is significant with regard to the graphic and, at times, obscene representation of libertine debauchery for the purposes of political and religious satire.

sexually. The 18th-century French philosopher Jean-Jacques Rousseau felt his first erotic thrill when spanked by his young governess. Moreover, sodomy was known to be widespread in the all-male *collèges* of the time. It was his uncle's extensive library, however, to which he had access during his stays at the family château of Saumane in Provence, that aroused the youngster's interest in the radical thought of the time and in the literary representation of sex. This library contained works by all the great classical authors, but it also included major volumes of

2. Van Loo portrait of the young Marquis de Sade, circa 1760–62

Enlightenment philosophy, and significantly, a wide range of libertine writings.

After a brief military career in the Seven Years' War, in the course of which Sade distinguished himself in action, he embarked upon a life of pleasure in Paris, where he regularly frequented the theatres, avidly watching all the fashionable plays and falling in and out of love with the leading actresses. The Marquis was a good-looking young man with an exceptional ability to charm the ladies, and these passions were no doubt frequently reciprocated. Concerned to put a stop to Donatien's dissolute lifestyle and anxious to find a good wife for him, his father, himself practically destitute, quickly came up with a plan for him to marry a young woman from a recently ennobled but, more importantly, rich and influential family, the Montreuils. After a number of delays, not the least of which was occasioned by the discovery that Sade was suffering from a venereal disease, the wedding finally took place on 17 May 1763. Renée-Pelagie de Montreuil was no beauty but possessed many sterling qualities, chief among which were loyalty, steadfastness, and resilience, that would prove so invaluable in the years to come. Above all, Renée-Pelagie was clearly smitten with the dashing young nobleman and would remain utterly devoted to him for the next 27 years, in spite of the trials she would have to endure during her husband's long years in prison in the 1770s and 1780s.

Donatien's relationship with his mother-in-law, La Présidente de Montreuil, was at first extremely amicable. Like so many women in Sade's life, she was no doubt seduced by his charming ways and flattered by his attentions. The young Sade actively pursued his interest in the theatre at this time, staging plays in which he regularly cast La Présidente in a leading role.

Just five months after the wedding, however, the impetuous young noble was arrested for the crime of debauchery and imprisoned at Vincennes. Sade had shocked a young Parisian prostitute with talk of masturbating into chalices and thrusting communion hosts into vaginas, and frightened her with whips and other weapons. This first period of imprisonment, in 1763, lasted only three weeks, but the incident that occasioned it was just the beginning of a libertine career that was to last another fourteen years.

During this time, Sade certainly committed a number of similar acts that some might now consider reprehensible, acts that included the flagellation and buggery of prostitutes, and, allegedly, the sexual corruption of young women, although there is no reason to believe that any of this behaviour involved compulsion.

In 1768, a 36-year-old beggar-woman from Alsace named Rose

3. **The Château de La Coste. La Coste was the marquis's favourite of the Sade family properties. It is situated in Provence at the foot of the Lubéron hills on a hill-top overlooking the delightful ancient village of the same name. It was here that Sade at times sought refuge from the authorities. This was also the scene of a number of orgies involving young servant-girls.**

Keller accused Sade of subjecting her to acts of libertinage, sacrilege and sadism on Easter Sunday in his house at Arcueil. The marquis claimed she was a prostitute who had been well paid for her services and that he never intended her any harm. Nevertheless, he was imprisoned for six months initially at Saumur, then at Pierre-Encise near Lyons.

Four years later, in 1772, he and his valet held a party with a number of young prostitutes in Marseilles, following which one of the young women became seriously ill. The Marquis was suspected of having poisoned them, and the matter was reported to the authorities. In fact, although he may well have been guilty of buggery, Sade had merely given the prostitutes pastilles containing Spanish fly, a well-known aphrodisiac, with the intention of causing flatulence. Given

Sade's fixation on the female posterior, this effect undoubtedly gave him a perverse scatological thrill, although we cannot rule out the possibility that he would also have found the somewhat farcical consequences highly amusing. Sade was certainly not without a sense of humour, evidence of which can already be seen on this occasion in his swapping names with his valet.

Clearly, however, the dose of Spanish fly administered by Sade had been dangerously excessive. As the situation grew serious, the two men escaped to Italy, out of reach of the French authorities. They were accompanied briefly by Renée-Pelagie's beautiful sister, the 20-year-old Anne-Prospère, who had fallen for the Marquis's charms. With a remarkable lack of jealousy and sense of loyalty to her wayward husband, Renée-Pelagie remained in Provence to attempt to limit the damage by bribing two of the prostitutes to withdraw their charges. Nevertheless, Sade and his valet were condemned to death for crimes of sodomy (which was a capital offence in 18th-century France) and attempted poisoning, and the death sentence was carried out in absentia, their bodies symbolically burned in effigy at Aix. Mme de Montreuil never forgave her son-in-law for seducing her younger daughter and did all she could henceforth to have him placed and kept under lock and key.

On all the available evidence, Sade had no criminal intent in his encounters with prostitutes, whose services he employed undoubtedly because he had a high sex drive, hungered after novelty in the bedroom, and, not least, because his perverse liking for sodomy, flagellation, and coprophilia may have been just too extreme for the marital chamber. As to his reckless treatment of prostitutes in Marseilles and elsewhere, on the other hand, there is some indication in his correspondence of a nobleman's contempt for those 'vile creatures': why should a man of his rank suffer opprobrium and worse on the word of a mere whore who was well paid to satisfy her customer? Such attitudes obviously appear shocking now, but we should remember that they were commonplace among the 18th-century nobility. In this respect, the Marquis de Sade was no different from a great many of his aristocratic male contemporaries.

The early 1770s were marked by a protracted cat-and-mouse game with the authorities. Periods of imprisonment under *lettres de cachet* (which permitted detention without trial) alternated with brief interludes of freedom following a succession of Houdini-like escapes. Eventually, following his rearrest in February 1777, Sade began a 13-year-long period of incarceration, initially at Vincennes, then in the Bastille, to which he was transferred in February 1784. He was eventually released on April Fool's Day, 1790, when the *lettres de cachet* were abolished by the new revolutionary government. During his protracted period of imprisonment, Sade had composed an impressive number of literary works, including the infamous *One Hundred and Twenty Days of Sodom* which would be lost when he was moved from the Bastille days before it was stormed.

By the time of Sade's release, Renée-Pelagie, worn down by years of dogged devotion to Sade in his troubled times, had moved to a Paris convent where she resolved to spend the remainder of her days, refusing all further contact with her husband. The reasons for this separation are many and complex. During the long years of Sade's imprisonment, Renée had not felt able to abandon her husband. This would have felt like an act of betrayal at the worst of times, and in any case, there is much evidence in their personal correspondence of a continuing and mutual affection between man and wife. Indeed, Renée tended to all of Sade's needs, material and sexual, throughout his incarceration in Vincennes and the Bastille. However, bowing to the relentless pressure from her mother to sever all ties with her good-for-nothing spouse, and increasingly feeling the need to reconcile herself with God as she approached the age of 50, she was finally persuaded that a legal separation would be best. The turbulent events of the Revolution undoubtedly helped to spur Renée into taking this step, and the Paris convent offered the sanctuary she sought, both from her husband and the world.

In the summer of 1790, however, the ageing but resilient ex-aristocrat met Constance Quesnet, who would become his new lover and loyal companion. Constance, nicknamed 'Sensitive' by Sade on account of her highly strung temperament, was a 33-year-old former actress with a 6-year-old son. Sade would remain devoted to both of them, and they to him, for the rest of his life.

Citizen Louis Sade, as he was now obliged to style himself, given the risks associated with an aristocratic background, very quickly established a new career in the Revolution as a skilled political orator, becoming secretary of his revolutionary section for a brief period. In 1793, he was even appointed one of the section's judges, and later, in July of that year, he was elected president of his section, a position that he could easily have exploited to avenge himself on his in-laws for their opposition to his release from prison under the *ancien régime*. At the first meeting he chaired, it is recorded that Sade resigned his presidency in protest at a motion that came before the section. The Revolutionary Tribunal were arresting the parents of émigrés as counter-revolutionaries, and it is highly likely that the motion concerned the imposition of the death penalty on such people living in Sade's district. A vote in favour would have condemned Sade's in-laws to death, since they were themselves local residents and, with the exception of Renée-Pelagie, all of the Montreuils' children had emigrated. Although Sade's refusal undoubtedly saved the Montreuils' lives, it was in fact motivated far more by his own staunch opposition to the death penalty than by any charitable feelings towards a couple who had done their best to destroy him.

Such acts of political moderation, coupled with an unfashionable atheism and an aristocratic past that came back to haunt him, led inevitably to his arrest for 'counter-revolutionary activities' on

8 December 1793. He narrowly escaped the guillotine owing to a bureaucratic error and was released from prison on 15 October 1794 following the fall of Robespierre, the statesman whose influence during the period known as The Terror (see p. 53) had led to the arrest and execution of thousands of aristocrats and other 'enemies of the people'. Robespierre was himself guillotined in July 1794.

His lands and property having been seized during the Revolution, Sade was virtually penniless throughout the 1790s, leading a hand-to-mouth existence with Constance, and, for a while, reduced to working as a prompt in a Versailles theatre for 40 sous a day.

The 1790s saw the anonymous publication of Sade's major libertine works: *Philosophy in the Boudoir*, two novel-length versions of the *Justine* narrative, and the companion volume, *The Story of Juliette*. Sade was in part driven to publish these audacious works to generate much-needed funds. In fact, however, he never made much from them. On the contrary, he paid a heavy price for these obscene writings. Having been systematically hunted down as the author of the notorious *Justine*, Sade was finally arrested at his publishers' office on 6 March 1801, a copy of the newly printed *Juliette* in his hand.

After a brief spell in prison, he was moved to the more salubrious surroundings of the insane asylum at Charenton where he would remain until his death in 1814. Under the enlightened management of François de Coulmier, Charenton offered the ageing ex-Marquis a number of distinct advantages, not least of which was the opportunity to pursue his passion for the theatre. It is ironic that during this last phase of his life, when he once again found himself in captivity, Sade enjoyed greater freedom than ever before to write, perform plays, and even to indulge an undiminished taste for young women. Constance was moved into the asylum under the pretence that she was his daughter, and during the last two years of his life

DÉPARTEMENT DE LA SEINE.

CANTON DE CHARENTON.

COMMISSION ADMINISTRATIVE
DE L'HOSPICE CIVIL
DE CHARENTON-S.-MAURICE.

EXTRAIT du Registre des délibérations de la Commission Administrative de l'Hospice de CHARENTON-SAINT-MAURICE.

Séance du 29 Frimaire.

Les Administrateurs ont continué de s'occuper du régime intérieur de l'Hospice, et ils ont arrêté le Règlement, ainsi qu'il suit :

RÈGLEMENT.

ARTICLE PREMIER.

L'ARRÊTÉ du 19 frimaire dernier, contenant la nomination des divers Employés, leurs traitemens et leur nourriture, sera exécuté selon sa forme et teneur, à compter du premier nivôse prochain.

II.

L'ÉCONOME-RECEVEUR recevra tous les revenus de l'Hospice, et toutes les sommes qui lui sont ou pourront être dues; en donnera quittance, et, à défaut de payement, fera toutes les poursuites et diligences nécessaires pour contraindre les débiteurs.

Il achètera tous les comestibles, tous les médicamens, et autres choses nécessaires au service et approvisionnement de l'Hospice, qu'il ne payera que sur les mémoires et factures des Marchands, visés et ordonnancés par la Commission. Il fera tous les autres dépenses jugées nécessaires d'après les arrêtés de la Commission.

Il rendra compte de ses recettes et dépenses tous les trois mois, aux termes de l'article III de la loi du 16 vendémiaire dernier.

Il aura l'inspection et la surveillance générale pour le maintien du bon ordre et la tranquillité dans la maison; et en cas de trouble ou de manques essentiels au service des malades, il en référera à la Commission.

III.

LE SOUS-ÉCONOME secondera l'Économe dans toutes ses fonctions.

Il aura, en l'absence de l'Économe, la sous-inspection et surveillance générale pour le maintien de l'ordre, de la tranquillité et du service des malades.

Il sera chargé de tous les approvisionnemens, et distribuera suivant les ordres qui lui en seront donnés par l'Économe, ou d'après les ordonnances assignées de l'Officier de santé en chef, quant à ce qui concerne le service des malades.

IV.

LA GARDIENNE du linge, la rangera proprement et par espèces, et l'entretiendra de son mieux; elle le fera blanchir, en prenant la précaution de séparer le fin du gros, et de celui qui, ayant servi aux malades, se trouveroit gâté par les onguens. Elle inspectera les Blanchisseuses pour que le linge soit bien blanchi, et qu'il ne s'en perde pas; elle le distribuera suivant les ordres qu'elle en recevra de l'Économe ou du Sous-Économe, et aura soin de le faire remettre le linge sale. Elle aura la sous-surveillance dans la salle des femmes malades, et les Infirmières la seconderont dans tout ce qui concerne le service des malades femmes, sur lesquelles elle aura à veiller.

V.

L'OFFICIER de santé en chef aura son logement à l'Hospice, et s'en éloignera le moins possible, afin d'être toujours à portée de donner aux malades les secours dont ils peuvent avoir besoin.

Il remettra tous les jours, au premier pansement, à son Élève en chirurgie, un état signé de lui des médicamens et nourriture nécessaires à chaque malade. Les doses seront expliquées en toutes lettres, et non en signes, afin d'éviter toutes erreurs.

VI.

L'ÉLÈVE en chirurgie tiendra exactement les pansemens; il exécutera et fera exécuter par les Infirmiers et Infirmières les ordonnances de l'Officier de santé en chef; dont il prendra copie, et remettra les originaux à faire nôme ou du Sous-Économe, pour qu'ils les fassent aussi exécuter chacun en ce qui les concerne. Il ne pourra pas s'absenter, et n'aura une permission par écrit de l'Économe, ou en bas absence, du Sous-Économe, qui ne l'accorderont que sur celle de l'Officier de santé en chef; il rasera les malades.

VII.

LE CUISINIER et l'Aide de Cuisine ne délivreront de bouillon que sur les ordres de l'Économe et, en son absence, du Sous-Économe. Les bouillons étant spécialement réservés pour les malades. Il en sera de même de la viande et des légumes qu'ils ne délivreront que sur les ordres de l'Économe ou du Sous-Économe, qui indiqueront la quantité nécessaire aux malades, d'après la demande de l'Officier de santé.

VIII.

LE Jardinier et son Garçon entretiendront le jardin de toutes sortes de légumes, et surtout de gros. Ils ne le délivreront que sur les ordres de l'Économe ou du Sous-Économe, sans pouvoir en donner ni en vendre à quelque personne que ce soit, du dedans de l'Hospice ou du dehors; ils cueilleront les allées du jardin en bon état.

IX.

LES Infirmiers et Infirmières auront le plus grand soin des malades; ils les serviront avec douceur, et mettront la plus stricte exactitude et ponctualité à exécuter les ordonnances de l'Officier de santé en chef, et à faire ce qui, en son absence, leur sera demandé par l'Élève en chirurgie; ils ne pourront pas s'absenter des salles sans une permission par écrit de l'Économe, ou, en son absence, du Sous-Économe, qui ne l'accorderont que sur la demande des femmes; à moins que l'Économe, de concert avec l'Officier de santé, ne jugent qu'il suffit qu'une seule personne veille pour les malades, auquel cas elles veilleront seulement à leur tour, ainsi que les Infirmiers.

X.

LE Portier ne laissera sortir aucun malade de l'Hospice sans la permission par écrit de l'Économe ou du Sous-Économe. Cette permission restera entre ses mains pour être représentée au besoin; il ne laissera pareillement sortir

de l'Hospice aucun meuble, paquet ou effet quelconque, sans la même formalité.

XI.

LES pansemens des malades se feront toujours comme par le passé; en été à six heures du matin et à six heures du soir, en hiver à sept heures du matin et à quatre heures du soir.

Toutes les autres choses nécessaires aux malades en médicamens, nourriture, linge et autres objets, seront fournies, d'après les ordres de l'Économe ou du Sous-Économe, d'après la demande de l'Officier de santé en chef, qu'il ou qu'il ou dira ci-devant.

Aucunes autres personnes de l'intérieur ou du dehors de l'Hospice ne pourront donner ni vendre aux malades aucunes choses, non plus ni médicamens, nourriture ou boissons, à peine, ceux du dedans, d'être renvoyés, ceux du dehors de ne pouvoir plus rentrer à l'Hospice.

Défenses sont faites à toutes personnes, de vendre dans l'intérieur de l'Hospice, ni vins, ni liqueurs, à peine d'expulsion.

XII.

LES convalescens ne pourront rester à l'Hospice plus de huit jours, après leur entrée en convalescence, à moins d'un certificat de l'Officier de santé en chef, qui constate que la convalescence n'est pas assez avancée, et le nombre de jours nécessaires pour la perfectionner.

XIII.

LES malades ne feront aucun bruit, demanderont doucement aux Infirmiers les choses qui leur seront nécessaires, sauf, en cas de refus ou du devoir de la part des Infirmiers, à en porter leurs plaintes à l'Officier de santé, qui, en cas de gravité dans lesdites plaintes, en référera à l'Économe, et même aux Administrateurs.

XIV.

IL ne sera admis à l'Hospice que des malades de maladies curables, non contagieuses, ni produites par la débauche.

XV.

TOUS les malades, soit hommes, soit femmes, qui seront admis à l'Hospice, seront tenus de représenter, en y entrant, un certificat de l'Agent Municipal de leur Commune, qui contiendra leur nom propre, leurs prénoms, leur âge, le lieu de leur naissance, les noms et prénoms de leurs père et mère, et qui constatera de plus que celui qui se présente est pauvre, et hors d'état de se faire soigner.

Ces certificats étant principalement exigés pour l'instruction de l'Officier public, dans le cas où un malade viendroit à mourir à l'Hospice, ils resteront à la Commission tant que les malades seront à l'Hospice; ils le leur feront rendre à leur sortie, avec le visa d'un Administrateur.

LES Administrateurs visiteront les salles des malades, le plus souvent qu'ils le pourront.

Signés MAUGIS, *Président*; GANDOLPHE, *Secrétaire*; GOUAUX, ROZIER et LEDUC.

À CHARENTON-LE-PONT, de l'Imprimerie de J. - Cн. Lаvеаux, N°. 12.

---

4. Rules of the Charenton asylum, issued on the 29 Frimaire, Year V

there was a regular arrangement of a sexual nature with a 16-year-old girl named Madeleine Leclerc, daughter of an employee in the asylum laundry.

Sade died of a pulmonary condition on 2 December 1814 at the age of 74, and at the behest of his younger son, Armand, was buried with full Christian rights in the small asylum cemetery. No trace remains of his grave today.

Sade's literary output

Sade wrote an impressive amount during his 74 years. However, much of it has not survived. A number of manuscripts were confiscated and destroyed by the authorities during his time at Charenton, while others were burned after his death at the family's behest. Among the works that have endured until the present day are many conventionally written plays, stories, and verses, but Sade's sulphurous reputation rests upon those three obscene works that were already in the public domain in the 1790s (*Justine*, *Philosophy in the Boudoir*, and *Juliette*), together with *The 120 Days of Sodom*, the loss of which in the Revolution ironically preserved the work for posterity (see Chapter 5). Chapters 2, 5, and 6 of this book will be devoted to Sade's literary output, with special emphasis on these four libertine novels. Chapters 3 and 4 will focus on Sade's stance on religion and politics. A final chapter will attempt to assess Sade's intellectual, cultural, and moral legacy in the modern era.

As with the life, the work deserves to be assessed dispassionately. But if this brief review has any kind of agenda, it is to give the Marquis de Sade his place as a writer and thinker of originality, and not a little merit, in all of those literary histories and encyclopedias from which he has for so long been excluded and where he rightly belongs.

Chapter 2
Man of letters

Sade took his literary endeavours very seriously indeed, describing himself variously as dramatist, author, novelist, and, with characteristic self-importance, 'man of letters'. In this, as in so many other areas of his life, Renée-Pelagie lent him her whole-hearted support, reading first drafts and offering constructive advice, and sometimes even providing factual information requested by her husband for scene-setting in his novels.

He was active as a writer from his youth, composing occasional verses and travelogue-style accounts of his experiences as a young soldier. His *Journey to Holland* and *Journey to Italy*, for example, written in 1769 and 1776 respectively, were inspired by months spent travelling in these countries. As for Sade's theatrical interests, one of his earliest known plays, *The Would-be Philosopher*, was staged at La Coste in 1772. There is also some evidence that he wrote pornographic works as early as 1769 to make money. However, his writing activities really began in earnest in the Bastille during his first long period of imprisonment in the 1780s. By 1788, he had composed a sufficiently impressive quantity of work to feel able to draw up a *catalogue raisonné* of his literary output. This catalogue, which did not include any of his libertine writings, comprised no fewer than eight novels and volumes of short stories, sixteen historical novellas, two volumes of essays, a day-to-day diary, and an impressive portfolio of more than twenty plays. Of this canon of writings, only a small number survived the storming of the Bastille in 1789.

Sade's writing for the theatre was certainly not without merit, displaying a vast literary and historical culture, an intimate knowledge of theatre practice, and, above all, a profound sense of the dramatic. Yet, as we shall see in Chapter 5, it is in the libertine novels that Sade's theatrical gifts really come into their own.

All of the plays and the prose works listed in the catalogue are completely devoid of any obscenity and conform in every sense to the accepted literary norms of the age. On the other hand, in their total disregard for the conventions of form as well as their shocking content, the obscene works that Sade composed in the 1780s and 1790s are of considerably more interest than anything else he wrote. These are the four libertine novels: *The 120 Days of Sodom*, *Philosophy in the Boudoir*, *Justine*, and *Juliette*.

In addition to his output in the Bastille and during the revolutionary years of the 1790s, Sade composed four more novels in the last period of his life in the asylum at Charenton, of which only three have survived: *Adelaide of Brunswick, Princess of Saxony, The Secret History of Isabelle of Bavaria, Queen of France*, and *The Marquise of Gange* are all conventional historical narratives. The fourth, an unfinished manuscript entitled *The Days at Florbelle*, and Sade's only libertine novel of the period, was ordered to be burned after his death by his younger son, Donatien-Claude-Armand. Surviving author notes for this work suggest that Sade was attempting to recreate the lost *120 Days of Sodom*.

Short stories

Apart from the travelogues and diaries, Sade's early experiments in prose writing were largely confined to the genre of the *conte*, or short story. These tales are highly entertaining and reveal impressive literary skills. Above all, they display a real gift for story-telling. The first version of *Justine* (*The Misfortunes of Virtue*, 1787), for example, long enough to be considered a novella at about 150 pages, is still considerably shorter and far less ponderous than its novel-length reworkings – *Justine* (1791) and *The New Justine* (1797). Sade intended to publish other *contes* in a volume entitled *Tales and Fabliaux of the Eighteenth Century by a Provençal Troubadour*. Many of these stories combine bawdy humour with biting satire, for instance of the legal profession and the parlements. There are cuckolded husbands, prudish wives, and, in the *Justine* tale, scenarios in remote castles and sepulchral abbeys that appear Gothic in character – although as we shall see presently, the word 'Gothic' must be used with caution in relation to Sade.

The shorter tales were more playful. Indeed, Sade liked to think of himself as 'the French Boccaccio', an ambition suggested by the titles of many of these tales: 'The Windbags of Provence', 'The

The Gothic novel

The word 'Gothic' is taken to refer to the art and architecture of the Middle Ages. In the 18th century, the 'Gothic revival' in architecture was echoed in English literature, and the 'Gothic novel' became a dominant genre of the second half of the century. 'Gothic novels' had medieval settings, such as haunted castles or monasteries, and dealt with supernatural terrors and cruel passions. The best-known examples are Walpole's *Castle of Otranto* (1764), Ann Radcliffe's *Mysteries of Udolpho* (1794), and Matthew Lewis's *The Monk* (1795). Although not set in the Middle Ages, 19th-century works such as Mary Shelley's *Frankenstein* (1818) that have a gloomy or spine-chilling atmosphere are also regarded as belonging to the Gothic tradition.

Self-made Cuckold', 'The Pimp Well Served', 'The Obliging Husband', and so on.

This last story, which Sade reworked in another short tale, 'Let it be Done in the Prescribed Way', is an especially good example of Sade's comic gifts, but also of the originality of his approach to the moral tale, a dominant prose-fiction genre of the second half of the 18th century. In it, a nobleman, well known for his taste for sodomy, is to marry a young and naive virgin. Aware of the nobleman's sexual preferences, the girl's mother issues a warning to her the day before the wedding: 'beware of the first suggestion your husband makes to you and tell him firmly: "No, monsieur, that is not the way a decent woman does it, any other way that you like, but absolutely not that way . . . "'. On their wedding-night, however, the nobleman decides to show his new wife some consideration and offers to fulfil his marital duties in the conventional manner. But remembering her mother's caution, the bride objects:

'What do you take me for, monsieur? [. . .] In any other way that you like, but absolutely not that way.'

'Very well, madame, your wish shall be granted,' said the prince while taking possession of his cherished sanctum. 'I should be very sorry if it were said that I had ever set out to displease you.'

In this mischievous little tale, Sade stands the conventional moral lesson of the genre on its head and, at the same time, exploits the stock 'biter bit' scenario in a highly novel and uniquely Sadean fashion. He also characteristically undermines the authority of mothers over their daughters' sexuality.

On one important level, therefore, 'The Obliging Husband' is a clear parody of the moral tale. The triteness and sentimentality of the moral tale's themes were of course vulnerable to ironic treatment by those who, like Sade, were nauseated by the genre's celebration of virtue and *sensibilité*. In his essay 'Reflections on the Novel', Sade dismisses the tales of Jean-François Marmontel, an important exponent of the genre, as 'puerile nonsense, written only for women and children'.

This parodic recycling of the moral tale can also be traced through the collection of stories, *The Crimes of Love*, to which 'Reflections on the Novel' was prefaced. This collection did not appear until 1800, but all of the stories contained in it were composed much earlier, during Sade's period of imprisonment in the Bastille from 1787 to 1788. These tales were considerably darker in tone than the *Tales and Fabliaux*, drawing on some elements of the Gothic tradition in vogue at the time, and showing the awful and often fatal consequences of incestuous passion.

The influence of the Gothic novel's fondness for medieval settings and bloodcurdling crimes can certainly be found in the remote forests, monasteries, and castles of *Justine* and *The Crimes of Love*, and in the horrific crimes retailed in these stories, but fear of the supernatural and the accompanying dread of the night and of dark forbidding places so beloved of Gothic writers are completely absent from Sade's narratives. It would therefore be quite wrong to consider any of Sade's works as belonging to the Gothic genre, strictly defined.

The crime of incest, which is also an important leitmotif in the long novels, is in part, for Sade, a revolutionary response to the religious and moral order of a century in which the family was a sacred but often suffocating social unit. However, all forms of incest do not enjoy the same prominence in Sade's narratives, so that mother-son incest, for example, is comparatively rare, while father-daughter incest predominates. The treatment of the incest theme in *The Crimes of Love* tales is never obscene, unlike Sade's most notorious depiction of incest in *Philosophy in the Boudoir*, in which Eugénie penetrates her own mother's vagina and anus with a dildo, and in which, crucially, the mother is delivered into the daughter's hands by the father.

Possibly the best examples of Sade's representation of father-daughter incest in *The Crimes of Love* collection are to be found in 'Eugénie de Franval' and 'Florville et Courval'. These tales, of around 100 pages each, are typical of Sade's approach to the tragic short story, and contain many elements that we find considerably extended and developed in the novels.

In 'Eugénie de Franval', subtitled 'Tragic Novella', a father raises his own daughter with the sole aim of possessing her sexually. The narrative contains justifications of incest by reference to ancient usage, as well as a spirited defence by the daughter herself of her incestuous love for her father. Both the choice and the manner of representation of the theme of incest may clearly be read as rehearsals for later works, in particular *Philosophy in the Boudoir*, in which the enthusiastic young sexual novice is also named Eugénie.

In 'Florville and Courval', subtitled 'or Fatalism', the eponymous heroine is considerably less sanguine than Eugénie about her incestuous relations, all of which she enters into unwittingly. In an ironic inversion of the Oedipus legend, Florville is unknowingly responsible for the death of her mother and marries her own father after being seduced by her brother and her son, all the fateful consequences of circumstance.

Both tales pay lip-service to the moralizing conventions of the genre, while the praise of virtue and the condemnation of vice expressed by the narrator are directly undercut by the authoritative arguments in favour of libertinism delivered by leading characters. While the reader of 'Eugénie de Franval', for example, is grandly informed in the tale's opening paragraph that 'To educate men and correct their morals, such is our only motive in writing this story', the libertine Franval always seems to have the last word. When told that incest is against the law, he retorts: 'What folly! A pretty girl ought not to tempt me just because I made the mistake of bringing her into the world?', and in a debate with a priest, named Clervil, he demisses the moral imperatives of the scriptures and our conscience as culturally relative and therefore quite unreliable. Franval is finally punished for his sins, killing himself on his wife's coffin, but with his dying breath, he paints himself as the 'sad slave of his passions', a clue to the tale's fundamentally deterministic underlying message, suggested by the subtitle: we are all the victims of our biological make-up and cannot be blamed for what it is not in our power to control.

The novel

In the essay 'Reflections on the Novel' (1800), Sade reviews the novel genre from classical times up to the contemporary period. He gives special prominence to the troubadours of medieval Europe as the initiators of novelistic practice in France. There is a brief discussion of leading French and Spanish novels of the 16th and 17th centuries as a prelude to the essay's main purpose: an evaluation of 18th-century European novels in the light of his own practice as a novelist. This survey is partly designed to display Sade's erudition, but the combative tones of some passages make it above all a literary polemic. The predictable denial of authorship of *Justine*, found towards the end of the essay, plays an important role in Sade's campaign for literary respectability.

Three omissions in the list of authors discussed are initially perplexing. There is no mention of Denis Diderot's *The Nun* (1760; published 1796) or his *Jacques the Fatalist* (1773; published 1796), of Jacques-Henri Bernardin de Saint-Pierre's *Paul and Virginie* (1788), or of Pierre Choderlos de Laclos's *Dangerous Liaisons* (1782), all important milestones in the evolution of the French novel in the 18th century. However, Sade may have preferred to keep silent about novels whose undeniable qualities undermined his own claim to be the natural heir to a tradition stretching from the troubadours to Rousseau. He may also have been unwilling to discuss works of his own era whose plots and themes bore an uncomfortable resemblance to his own. Laclos's epistolary masterpiece is a brilliant portrait of libertine wickedness which may have directly inspired several of Sade's own compositions (*Aline and Valcour, Philosophy in the Boudoir*), and to acknowledge such a strong influence would obviously have undermined his own claims to originality. Sade's main aim in writing this essay was also to persuade the reader to take him seriously as a conventional writer, whereas Laclos's novel came dangerously close to definitions of libertine literature with which no serious author would have wished to be openly associated. This is why Sade is at such pains to scotch the rumours attributing *Justine* to himself, and why he makes only passing references to other libertine works. Only two libertine authors are mentioned: Claude Prosper Jolyot de Crébillon (Crébillon fils) merits no more than a line or two, and Restif de la Bretonne's works are summarily dismissed as 'terrible productions'. Sade and Restif de la Bretonne loathed each other intensely. Sade described Restif as a hack writer who churned out potboilers for money, while Restif called Sade a woman-hating monster and wrote *L'Anti-Justine* as a counterblast to *Justine*.

There is some doubt among scholars as to the exact date of publication of *The New Justine* and *Juliette*. What remains certain, however, is that the first published version of *Justine* sold extremely well throughout the 1790s and, despite its anonymity, is the work with which Sade's name was linked, both by critics and by the reading public. *Justine* is therefore the novel that he is at pains to repudiate, given his aspirations to be respected as a man of letters. Sade wished to be known as the author, not of *Justine*, but of the conventionally written *Aline and Valcour* (1795). Clearly, Sade sought to keep his public persona as a respectable author and his private passion for obscene compositions separate, not only for reasons of image and standing, but, more crucially, in order to avoid imprisonment under the harsh censorship laws of the new Napoleonic regime. As we have seen, his fears proved well-grounded.

The *Justine* affair

1787: Composition of the novella *The Misfortunes of Virtue* in the Bastille.

1791: Anonymous publication of the novel-length *Justine, or the Misfortunes of Virtue*.

1797–9: Anonymous publication of *The New Justine, or the Misfortunes of Virtue*, followed by the *History of Juliette, her Sister, or the Prosperities of Vice*.

18 August 1800: The police seize a new edition of *Justine*.

22 October 1800: Reviewing the recently published *The Crimes of Love*, the critic Villeterque accuses Sade of being the author of *Justine* and a threat to public morals.

6 March 1801: Sade's arrest at his publishers' for the authorship of obscene writings.

Among the novelists Sade does mention, there is praise for Boccaccio, Cervantes, Mme de Lafayette, Marivaux, Richardson, Fielding, Prévost, Crébillon, Voltaire, and especially Rousseau (and contempt for the improbabilities of the English Gothic novel). He then proceeds to lay down rules of good practice for the aspiring writer – there is considerable hypocrisy here, since he broke all of them himself:

- the novelist must strive to be convincing, if not truthful (his own novels are filled with improbable and even surreal elements);
- he must not interrupt the main plot with tangential episodes or narrative diversions (the Sade narrative is typically fragmented in structure and regularly punctuated with lengthy dissertations);

On the pleasures of pain
Example of the Sadean dissertation:

The truth is generally recognized: encourage or allow the object which serves for your pleasure to take enjoyment therein, and straightway you discover that it is at your expense; there is no more selfish passion than lust; none that is severer in its demands; smitten stiff by desire, 'tis with yourself you must be solely concerned, and as for the object that serves you, it must always be considered as some sort of victim, destined to that passion's fury. Do not all passions require victims? Well then! In the lustful act the passive object is that of our lubricious passion; spare it not if you would attain your end; the intenser the sufferings of this object, the more entire its humiliation, its degradation, the more thorough will be your enjoyment. They are not pleasures you must cause this object to taste, but impressions you must produce upon it; and that of pain being far keener than that of pleasure, it is beyond all question preferable that the commotion produced in our nervous system by this external spectacle be created by pain rather than by pleasure.

(Extract from Noirceuil's three-page
dissertation on pain, *Juliette*, p. 269)

- he should avoid the 'affectation' of moralizing – only the characters are permitted to make moral statements, and then only if circumstances require them to do so (the whole purpose of the numerous and lengthy dissertations delivered by characters in *Justine* and *Juliette*, and often supported by detailed authorial footnotes, is to comment on moral, religious, as well as political issues);
- he should not adhere slavishly to rules (the structures of *The*

120 Days of Sodom, in particular, are dictated by an obsessive preoccupation with symmetry and numbers).

Two essential principles underpin all these rules: the writer must be personally inspired and must reflect Nature's laws. Both principles can be seen to be based on Sade's own experience. The misfortune that dogged most of his adult life, it is implied, at least provided him with deeper insight into the human heart.

As for Nature's laws, they justify the portrayal of vice as triumphant over virtue, another marked feature of Sade's own novels. But Sade also justifies this approach on aesthetic and moral grounds. Firstly, the representation of vice triumphant makes for a more interesting read than the sentimentality of the Marmontel approach, according to which virtue must always be seen to prevail. Indeed, Sade here follows the ancient and respected tradition of Greek tragedy, in which pity and terror are evoked to cathartic effect. Secondly, by painting vice in true colours, he will rid his reader of any desire to associate with it. This latter justification may be thought to be not a little hypocritical, given Sade's belief in the essential role of evil in the order of things.

Critic wars

The Crimes of Love and its accompanying essay 'Reflections on the Novel' were the first of Sade's works to be published under his own name, and the hypocrisies of the text, the absence in it of any overtly obscene material, and, above all, his vigorous denial of authorship of the infamous *Justine*, all transparently serve Sade's aim of establishing himself as a respectable man of letters. At least one critic, however, was not fooled. A journalist named Villeterque condemned the collection as

> A detestable book by a man suspected of having written one even more horrifying [...] What possible utility is there in these portraits of crime triumphant? [...] I could not read these four volumes of revolting atrocities without indignation.

Sade found this attack so wounding that he felt compelled to compose a 20-page defence, entitled 'The Author of the Crimes of Love to Villeterque, Hack', and in which he compared the journalist's views with 'the morning cackling of barnyard animals' and vehemently denied having written *Justine*. The pamphlet rubbished Villeterque as a lying and defamatory hack-writer, and the tone was dismissive and contemptuous. Gilbert Lely's description of Sade's diatribe as 'A grand seigneur's cane brought down repeatedly on the back of an insolent lackey' is most apt. Clearly, the former Marquis had lost none of his aristocratic sense of superiority.

Letters and numbers

Alongside the short stories and the long novels Sade composed during his period of imprisonment from 26 August 1778 until his liberation in 1790, he also wrote a great many letters, which shed much light onto Sade's mental states and his relations with others – although, given the Marquis's tendency to play roles, they can never be taken at face value. Indeed, this correspondence also offers the literary critic invaluable insights into Sade's approach to the writing of fiction, from which it is not entirely distinct.

Most of these letters were addressed to his wife, Renée-Pelagie, though even letters to others, such as his notary, had to pass through her hands. All of these letters were strictly censored by the police, who frequently expurgated passages they found unacceptable. However, both Sade and his wife employed a variety of means to evade this censorship. They would write in invisible ink, adding between the lines a secret text written in lemon juice, or else they would use a coded language, full of allusions, *sous-entendus*, ambiguous expressions, and pseudonyms. This experience had a number of beneficial influences on Sade's development as a writer.

In particular, he shows a remarkable insight into the potential for any text to possess unconscious levels that seems to prefigure

Freud's theories by well over a century. He declares in a letter to Renée in May 1779:

> The simplest of all secrets, which I believe is well known to every twelve-year-old schoolboy, is that when one crosses out a line, the deleted line becomes the meaningful one in any passage [. . .]

When Sade comes to write fiction, it is perhaps this obsession with coding and concealment that leads him to build areas of secrecy into the narrative, in order to excite the reader and himself, just as he had in the letters he wrote from prison. Sade, the consummate story-teller, has doubtless realized that every successful narrative contains elements of mystery, a space defined by absence and yet, like the censored prison letters, retaining the marks of what has been erased. It was in prison that Sade learned the power of the hidden in language.

Initially, however, such devices were both the cause and effect of his paranoia. Sade became convinced that his release-date had already been fixed, and that not only his jailers but also his wife knew this date. He began to believe that Renée was attempting to communicate the information to him in her letters by means of signs and codes, in particular by the coded use of numbers.

This paranoia inevitably affected Sade's mental and psychological states, and in the early weeks and months of his imprisonment, his moods alternated between dark despair and cheerful optimism. Most of the time, though, he was able to retain an ironic distance from his situation that was not without a certain dry humour, even when complaining bitterly about his living conditions:

To Madame de Sade, 4th October, 1778

[. . .]

As for my cell, *'tis a very great act of dishonesty* was done me when

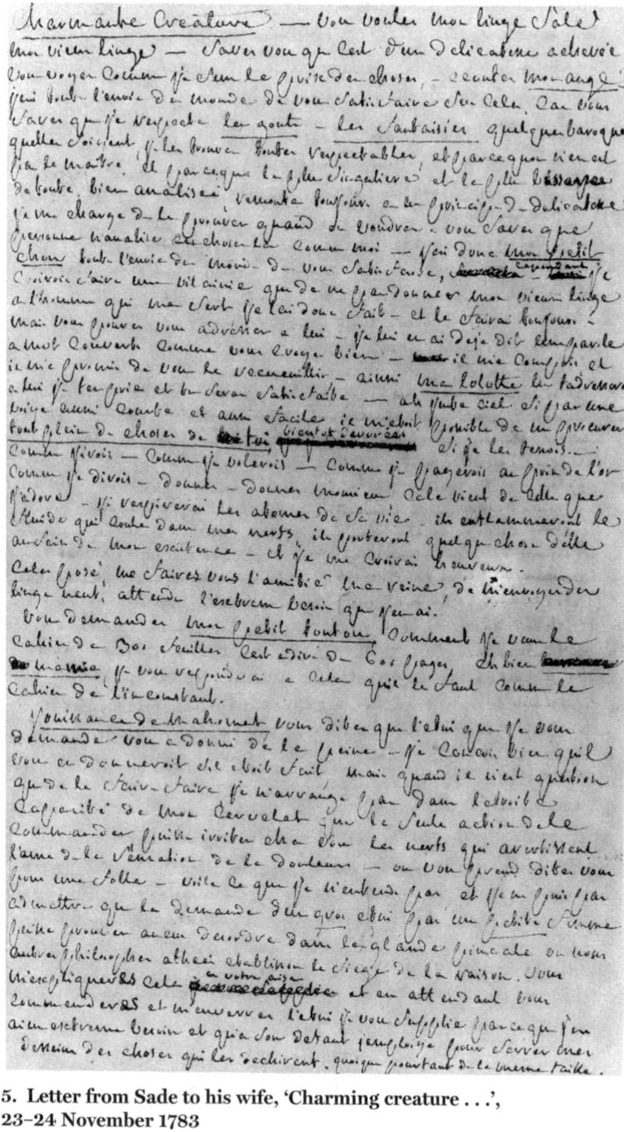

5. Letter from Sade to his wife, 'Charming creature . . .', 23–24 November 1783

mine was changed. 'Tis one more act to add to the others, and one I shall remember. Not only shall I be unable to have a fire throughout the winter, but, to boot, I am devoured by rats and mice, which keep me from getting a single minute of rest all night long. I have just spent six sleepless nights in a row, and when I ask if they would kindly have a cat put into the next room to destroy them, they answer that animals are forbidden. To which I respond: 'Why, fools that you are, if animals are forbidden, rats and mice should be forbidden, too.' To which they reply: 'That's different.'

When one reads the letters Sade wrote to his wife over 13 years, on the other hand, one cannot help but be struck by the sincerity of his love and affection for her. Admittedly, there are times when he loses patience with her and, on occasions, his paranoia leads him to suspect her of infidelity with other men. For the most part, however, much of the correspondence with Renée-Pelagie is concerned either with securing release from prison or else with his material requirements. At worst, Sade berates her for not sending him exactly what he has requested. These letters are punctuated by frequent pleas for paper and pens, but also for food, wines, rich delicacies, and especially chocolate. Then there are Sade's sexual needs. In a famous letter he wrote from Vincennes after seven years of imprisonment, entitled 'Vanilla and Manilla', he seems to combine his two favourite activities: eating and sex. 'Vanilla' was a code word for aphrodisiacs intended to improve the quality of his orgasms, while 'manilla' was his personal euphemism for masturbation. To increase his pleasure and assist his orgasms further, Sade had commissioned his wife to have dildos tailor-made for insertion into his anus.

The 'Vanilla and Manilla' letter is remarkable for the simplicity and precision with which Sade describes to his wife his sexual activities in prison, and in particular his extreme difficulty in ejaculating, which was probably due to a venereal disease or prostate infection. It also illustrates the use of codes and allusive references to evade the censor:

6. Letter from Sade to his wife, 'Vanilla and Manilla', 1784

I know full well that *vanille* causes overheating and that one should use *manille* in moderation. But what do you expect? When that is all one has […] One good hour in the morning for *five manilles*, artistically graduated from 6 to 9, a good half hour in the evening for three more […]

Sade uses two more code words to describe his problems

reaching climax: 'bow' and 'arrow' to designate his penis and semen:

> [. . .] nor is it because the bow is not taut – oh, don't worry, on that score it is everything you could hope for as far as rigidity goes – but the arrow refuses to leave the bow and that is the most exasperating part – because one wants it to leave – lacking an object, one goes slightly crazy [. . .] and 'tis for this reason I tell you that prison is bad, because solitude gives added strength only to ideas [. . .]

We note how Sade must have increasing recourse to his imagination ('ideas') in search of sexual satisfaction; how, in other words, his sexual frustration in prison provides an important impetus for the composition of those libertine fictions, all of which were begun in the Bastille. The exceptional nature of Sade's sexual appetites is evidenced by the remarkable number of anal masturbations he engaged in over two and a half years: 6,536, or more than seven a day, a figure recorded by the Marquis himself. Such a high level of auto-eroticism suggests both a powerful sexual imagination and a rare physical capacity for a man in his middle years.

In letters to his valet, Carteron, with whom he enjoyed what we would now call a laddish camaraderie, Sade displays a rumbustious and bawdy sense of humour. The tone is always one of affectionate and ribald berating. Note here Sade's incomparable talent for verbal obfuscation, designed partly to confuse the censor but no doubt also to amuse his correspondent:

October 4th, 1779

[. . .]

What, you good-for-nothing monkey, with your face of a scrub brush smeared with brambleberry juice, you pole in Noah's vineyard, you rib in the belly of Jonah's whale, you used matchstick, from a bordello's tinderbox ... you evil-smelling ha'penny candle, you rotten cinch from my wife's donkey ... what, you've found me no islands? You dare tell me that, you and your four comrades of the frigate sailing the shores around the port of Marseilles, you've not made the least effort to discover me any islands and you've not found me seven of them in the space of a morning? Ah: you old pumpkin pickled in bug juice, you third horn on the devil's head, you cod face with two oysters for ears, you old worn-out shoe of a bawd, you dirty linen full of Milli Springtime's red unmentionables, ah: if I had my hands on you now, how I'd rub your dirty face in them, that baked apple of yours that looks for all the world like a burning chestnut, to teach you not to tell such lies.

The 'islands' in question is probably a veiled reference to the Marseilles prostitutes who had brought charges of poisoning against Sade and so were responsible for his imprisonment on grounds of attempted murder and sodomy.

Sade's mental state obviously suffered from the long periods of solitary confinement to which he was subjected. The effects of this confinement were nevertheless positive as well as negative. On the negative side, his paranoid tendencies were heightened to the extent that he became convinced that Mme de Montreuil, his mother-in-law, was waging a general campaign against him and was singlehandedly responsible for his plight. Relations that had previously basked in mutual admiration were now irretrievably embittered: 'In truth, Mme de Montreuil wishes my ruin and that of my children . . . . ' he had written to his lawyer Gaufridy as early as autumn 1775:

That dreadful creature, through a charm (which she received from the devil, to whom she doubtless leagued her soul) that casts an inconceivably powerful spell on others, overpowers all that she touches . . . . [. . .] As long as I am not rehabilitated, not a cat in the province will be whipped without everyone saying, 'It's the Marquis de Sade's doing.'

Two years later, in letters to his wife, Sade is far less circumspect when expressing his feelings about Mme de Montreuil: she is now described as 'your whore of a mother', 'a brothel-keeper', 'a venomous beast', 'an infernal monster'.

The obsessive character of Sade's reactions to imprisonment is clear from the incredible volume of correspondence he produced – some 20 pages a day at this early stage in his captivity at the end of the 1770s. Haunting these letters week by week, Mme de Montreuil ends up as a kind of prototype for all the female victims of his fictions, the principal focus of his venom and hatred. At the same time, there are self-consciously ironic, if not blackly humorous, undertones in much of this anti-Montreuil rhetoric. Like some modern stand-up comic telling tasteless mother-in-law jokes, Sade inveighs against La Présidente with a regularity and a hyperbole that is self-consciously theatrical, as in these smouldering lines penned in February 1783: 'This morning, in the midst of my suffering, I saw her skinned alive, dragged over thistles, and then tossed into a vat of vinegar.'

On the positive side, as the above examples suggest, Sade's letters are written with an openness that is extraordinary for the time, and certainly considered by some as freer than anything composed before the Romantic period. They also display a remarkable stoicism and a self-ironizing sense of humour that one cannot help admire, given the circumstances of their composition. Many of the letters, moreover, have considerable literary merit, as the above examples suggest. Letter-writing fulfilled a number of different functions for Sade: much-needed therapy; a positive activity to wile away those long hours of confinement; a discourse with himself; and, of course, the main form of communication with the outside world. And as documentary evidence of the Marquis's changing states of mind during his time in prison, the letters are unique in the Sade canon of writings, offering an invaluable resource to scholars and the interested general reader alike.

Prison literature

The amount of correspondence Sade wrote during this time is quite simply astonishing, and the number of literary works produced within the gloomy walls of the Bastille was impressive by any standards, but it was not just a matter of quantity. Many of the letters, as we have seen, display a comic verve and a writer's gift for observation, while there is no doubting the very real literary merits of the *contes*. Indeed, he is considered by critics to be a key figure in the development of the short story at the end of the 18th century. As for those long novels that made his sulphurous reputation, perhaps if Sade had not suffered such a protracted period of imprisonment, they might never have been composed at all; without the desires that captivity made impossible to fulfil in reality, Sade would not have felt compelled to satisfy them vicariously in the fantasies of his libertine fictions.

Chapter 3
Martyr of atheism

If atheism wants martyrs, let it say so and my blood is ready.

The sheer radicality of Sade's atheism should not be underestimated. At a time when anti-religious sentiments and activities might attract a death sentence – on 1 July 1766, the 20-year-old Chevalier de la Barre was decapitated in Paris for so-called sacrilegious acts – it is not hard to understand why many of those who shared Sade's free-thinking tendencies were far more circumspect. Voltaire, for example, found an uneasy compromise in deism, while Rousseau clung to a naively optimistic faith in the benevolence of nature. Even the materialists Julien Offroy de La Mettrie and Claude-Adrien Helvétius, in whose work Sade found much of his inspiration, avoided any direct public statement of an atheism they undoubtedly embraced in private. Similarly, the philosophically radical authors of the *Encyclopédie*, Denis Diderot and Jean Le Rond d'Alembert, felt obliged to condemn atheism outright.

In that Sade does indeed live and die according to his beliefs, his description of himself as a martyr of atheism is, therefore, not entirely inaccurate. It is not merely religious dogma that he rejects, but all of the social and moral interdictions that derive from it, and it is for having transgressed these interdictions that Sade spent the best part of his adult life in prison, although nowadays, with the

7. Engraving for the first illustrated edition of *La nouvelle Justine*

exception of the rough treatment of prostitutes, the offences he committed (blasphemy, sodomy, and the publication of obscene works containing atheistic ideas) would hardly be considered crimes.

Sade's atheistic thinking was heavily influenced by the work of two materialist philosophers of the Enlightenment: La Mettrie's *Man Machine* (1748) and Paul-Henri Dietrich d'Holbach's *System of Nature* (1770). For the materialists there was no soul or spirit, everything in the universe being physical matter. La Mettrie held that human beings can be defined only by scientific observation. Man is thus quite simply a machine, subject to the laws of mechanical motion. Anticipating Freud's pleasure principle by more than a century, the materialists concluded that pleasure was the sole purpose of existence. Sade's libertine characters never tire of rehearsing both the theory and the practice of this doctrine. For Baron d'Holbach, we are nothing more than a collection of atoms, and even our conscience takes a material form. We cannot therefore have free will, since the human organism is driven by personal interest in all things, and morality just comes down to social utility or pragmatism. Sade declared that his whole philosophy was founded on d'Holbach's *System of Nature*, a book he would be prepared to die for.

[. . .] *The System of Nature* is verily and indubitably the basis of my philosophy, and I am and shall remain a faithful disciple of that philosophy even at the cost of my life, if it came to that. [. . .] a book that I recommended to the Pope himself, a golden book in a word, a book that ought to be in every library and whose tenets should be in the heads of everyone, a book that undermines and destroys forever the most dangerous and most odious of all fantasies, the one that has caused more bloodshed here on earth than any other, one against which the entire universe should rise up and destroy once and for all, if the people who make up this universe had the slightest idea of what constitutes their true happiness and tranquillity. . . . theism cannot for a moment stand up to the slightest scrutiny, and one would have to be completely ignorant of the workings of Nature not to recognize that it operates on its own and without any primary cause, and that so-called primary cause, which explains nothing and which on the contrary requires explanation, is naught but the *nec plus ultra* of ignorance.

(Letter to his wife, late November 1783)

Imitation being the sincerest form of flattery, he took whole passages from *The System of Nature* more or less verbatim and placed them in the mouths of his libertines as they attacked one religious dogma after another. Despite these plagiarisms, however, Sade adds elements to this materialist philosophy that are peculiarly his own. Particularly original and certainly striking is his theory of 'isolisme', according to which each human being is utterly alone in the universe. Noirceuil in *Juliette* expresses this idea succinctly, when he declares that 'all creatures are born isolated and with no need whatsoever for one another'. This pessimistic notion helps to explain the relative absence of fraternal sympathy in his work and the self-interest that alone motivates his libertine protagonists, and it represents a self-conscious inversion of Rousseau's belief in Man's innate sociability and fellow-feeling. In this perspective, there is no society worthy of that name, that is, one that functions in accordance with shared ethical and moral principles, observing what Rousseau called 'the general will'. As Friedrich Wilhelm Nietzsche would argue a hundred years later, if there is no God, there can be no pre-established moral values, and society, if it exists at all, does so in tension with the desires of its individual citizens.

> The equality prescribed by the Revolution is simply the weak man's revenge upon the strong; it's just what we saw in the past, but in reverse; that everyone should have his turn is only meet. And it shall be turnabout again tomorrow, for nothing in Nature is stable and the governments men direct are bound to prove as changeable and ephemeral as they.
>
> (Juliette, p. 120, authorial footnote)

Sade's libertines justify this self-interest as their sole guiding principle on the grounds that it is 'natural'. For in Nature, they argue, there is no distinction between individuals, but the strong always survive at the expense of the weak. Darwinian *avant la lettre*, Sade sees the domination of the weak by the strong as a universal natural law, designed to maximize the health and promote the survival of the species. Thus, when the strong exploit the weak, they are merely conforming to natural laws. By the same token, laws whose purpose is to protect the weak undermine Nature's plan. In the absence of any god, the only governing force in Sade's universe is Nature, and conventional, religion-based morality, as Nietzsche and Fyodor Dostoevsky were to conclude at the end of the 19th century, can have no meaning in such a universe, since there is no deity to define absolutes of right and wrong. No universal moral laws, then, only traditions and values that vary from century to century, from culture to culture. In such an uncertain moral climate, our only guide can be our reason, which is itself unreliable because heavily influenced by physical needs and sensations.

> All moral effects are to be related to physical causes, unto which they are linked most absolutely: the drumstick strikes the taut-drawn skin and the sound answers the blow: no physical cause, that is, no collision, and of necessity there's no moral effect, that is, no noise.
>
> (*Juliette*, p. 15)

Sade's most original contribution to the materialist tradition lies precisely in this: that he draws the logical and extreme conclusion from a philosophy that elevates the body to the exclusive source of everything that is human.

> Frequently we hear the passions declaimed against by unthinking orators who forget that these passions supply the spark that sets alight the lantern of philosophy; who forget that 'tis to impassioned men we owe the overthrow of all those religious idiocies wherewith for so long the world was plagued. 'Twas nought but the fires of emotion cindered that odious scare, the Divinity, in whose name so

many throats were cut for so many centuries; passion alone dared obliterate those foul altars. Ah, had the passions rendered man no other service, is this one not great enough to make us indulgent toward the passions' mischievous pranks?

(Juliette, p. 88)

Reason is above all subordinated to sexual desire, which must be paramount in all human behaviour. Since Nature does not itself obey any superior force, its workings are completely arbitrary, and this arbitrariness elicits an ambivalent response from Sade's protagonists. On the one hand, Nature is an ally because she justifies all his crimes, including murder (which is not actually a crime because it is necessary to the maintenance of balance in the natural order). On the other hand, the total lack of rationale behind Nature's effects is perceived by the libertine as a disturbing absence. Mother Nature is therefore an absent mother, resented for her neglectfulness – a 'bad breast', in the psychoanalytical perspective of Melanie Klein, that he longs to suckle and simultaneously feels impelled to destroy, to punish for her lack of reason or compassion. At the very least, Sadean Man yearns to equal Nature's power, but this power is infinite, and so he, too, must strive for infinity. This quest for infinity, for a transcendence that will enable him to best Nature, informs Sade's fictional writings at a number of levels, and is especially apparent in the themes and motifs of *Juliette*, which swarms with libertines of each gender who yearn to commit the ultimate crime: the destruction of the entire universe.

Oh, if I could set the universe on fire, I should still curse nature for offering only one world to my fiery desires!

(Clairwil in Juliette, p. 958; translation modified)

Dialogue between a Priest and a Dying Man

Of all the direct expressions of atheism in Sade's work, the *Dialogue between a Priest and a Dying Man* is probably the most incisive and, at the same time, the most artistically satisfying. One of

Sade's earliest compositions, this brief anti-religious polemic was composed in the Bastille in the summer of 1782 when he was also working on *The 120 Days of Sodom*. The influence of Sade's Jesuit training in rhetorical debate is the mainspring of this brilliant dramatic essay, which, as its title suggests, is not so much theatre as philosophical dialogue. But what makes the work charming as well as persuasive is the impish humour that lies behind its characters and situation.

When bidden by a priest to repent the many sins he has committed in his lifetime, a dying man retorts that he does indeed repent, not for having sinned, but for not having sinned enough. Had he acknowledged Nature's omnipotence and the necessity of all her laws, he would have made better use of the faculties Nature gave him to serve her: 'I only plucked an occasional flower when I might have gathered an ample harvest of fruit.'

In the ensuing dialogue, the moribund libertine deftly exposes the absurdity of each successive point put forward by the stooge cleric in defence of religious belief. These arguments are the standard theological responses to those thorny questions concerning the existence of evil, the mysteries of faith, the conflicts caused by religious differences, and life after death. As the dying man's arguments illustrate in a condensed form the most important elements of Sade's atheistic philosophy, it is worth briefly summarizing them here.

- If God created everything, he must also have created good and evil. The Church's argument that God does so in order to give Man the freedom to choose is absurd:

  . . . to what purpose, since from the outset, he knew the course affairs would take, and since, all-mighty as you tell me he is, he had but to make his creature choose as suited him?

- Where the priest seeks refuge in the mysteries of religion, the dying man claims that truth is simplicity:

  What need have you of a second difficulty when you are unable to resolve the first [...]? [...] he who blindfolds himself must surely see less of the light than he who snatches the blindfold away from his eyes. You compose, you construct, you dream, you magnify and complicate; I sift, I simplify.

- It is not possible to believe in what one does not understand:

  [...] understanding is the very lifeblood of faith; where understanding has ceased, faith is dead.

- Nature is perfectly autonomous and no supernatural force is needed to explain it. If there are vices as well as virtues, it is because Nature deems them both necessary, and so Man cannot be held responsible for his so-called crimes:

  There is not a single virtue which is not necessary to Nature and conversely not a single crime which she does not need and it is in the perfect balance she maintains between the one and the other that her immense science consists; but can we be guilty for adding our weight to this side or that when it is she who tosses us on to the scales?

This recurrent argument in Sade's writings holds that there are really no crimes, since all human behaviour is willed by Nature, including all sexual impulses and even murder. Sade thus shows himself to be a thorough-going philosophical determinist for whom human beings are the helpless and innocent 'pawns of an irresistible force'.

- The miraculous is not demonstrable as proof of God's existence. The miracles of Jesus, for example, are rejected as the vulgar tricks of an imposter:

before I'd be persuaded of the truth of a miracle I would have to be very sure the event so called by you was absolutely contrary to the laws of Nature, for only what is outside of Nature can pass for miraculous; and who is so deeply learned in Nature that he can affirm the precise point where her domain ends, and the precise point where it is infringed upon?

• Why should the Christian God be any truer than all of the other Gods to be found in different countries and cultures?:

Jesus is no better than Mohammed, Mohammed no better than Moses, and the three of them combined no better than Confucius, who did after all have some wise things to say while the others did naught but rave.

• Religion simply causes trouble:

[. . .] the mere name of these horrors has caused greater loss of life on earth than all other wars and all other plagues combined.

• One cannot be persuaded by the promise of Heaven or the threat of Hell because there is no afterlife, a thought that is more consoling than terrifying. In any case, Nature itself through its perpetual regenerations offers a kind of immortality:

Nothing perishes in the world, my friend, nothing is lost; man today, worm tomorrow, the day after tomorrow a fly; is it not to keep steadily on existing?

The dénouement of this mini-drama aims to eradicate any surviving religious sensibilities in the reader by exposing the hypocrisy of the clergy. The libertine tells him that sensual pleasures have always been dearer to him than all else, and that he wishes to end his life in their bosom: 'my end draws near, six women lovelier than the light of day are waiting in the chamber adjoining.' The dying man invites the priest to join him, and in a shocking reversal of roles, the libertine converts the priest, who abandons religious piety for physical pleasure. We note the cynical humour of the author-narrator's concluding observation, and, of course, the pre-eminent role accorded to bodily desires:

> The dying man rang, the women entered; and after he had been a little while in their arms the preacher became one whom Nature has corrupted, all because he had not succeeded in explaining what a corrupt nature is.

The Dialogue between a Priest and a Dying Man is an early example of what was to become a dominant theme in all of Sade's writings: a sustained campaign against religion, characterized by a bitterness that seems deeply personal in its intensity. It seems paradoxical that, while religion is the object of such hatred in Sade's texts, it should occupy so much space in the libertine novels in particular, manifesting itself notably in the transgressive pleasures that the libertines derive from blaspheming. At the height of their sexual excitement, the libertines often taunt God with obscenities, challenging the non-existent deity to confound them by hurling a thunderbolt from heaven to punish them for their sins. The true, hidden purpose of such challenges is to force God to break his silence. In fact, if he doesn't exist, there's no point in insulting him. When told that God sees his crimes, Moberti's response in *Juliette* is revealing:

> 'Peugh, I don't give a fuck about that witness! [. . .] I am only sorry that no God really exists, sorry, that is, to be deprived of the pleasure of insulting him more positively.'
>
> (*Juliette*, p. 1093; translation slightly modified)

Like the female body for the Sadean libertine, God is simultaneously an object of intense fascination and of immeasurable contempt.

These ambivalent attitudes to religion, so graphically expressed in the libertines' obsessive preoccupation with blasphemy, might therefore suggest an unconscious process of denial. After all, the need to keep repeating one's refusal to believe in X implies doubt as to X's non-existence. Some have consequently interpreted this preoccupation with God's existence psychoanalytically as evidence of religious belief that has been inverted or repressed but is nevertheless still present.

Others have challenged the hypothesis of a 'negative' theology in Sade, preferring to see Sade's repeated defence of atheism as a necessarily vigorous response to the entrenched and oppressive theism of his society and to the threat posed by the concept of a deity to intellectual freedom. At a time when the free thinker was regarded as a dangerous subversive, suffering persecution that often involved imprisonment, torture, and even execution, Sade's instincts as both rebel and iconoclast impelled him to speak out. As for blasphemy, the consummate libertine Dolmancé in *Philosophy in the Boudoir* defends this as an essential component of sexual pleasure:

> [...] as of the moment God does not exist, what's the use of insulting his name? but it is essential to pronounce hard and foul words during pleasure's intoxication, and the language of blasphemy very well serves the imagination [...] they must scandalize to the last degree; for 'tis sweet to scandalize [...]
>
> (p. 251)

Dolmancé here defines the pleasures of transgression, which for the 20th-century French author Georges Bataille is an essential component of all erotic activity: forbidden fruit always tastes sweeter. Religion represented the most ready source of the taboo in the 18th century. When the libertine masturbates onto the host that has in the mass become the body of Christ, he is aiming to perform the most shocking act conceivable in order to achieve the greatest sexual thrill. Clearly, one can only transgress a taboo that one acknowledges, but in Sade's case, this is less a religious than a psychological process, less a matter of infringing moral laws or committing sins that can only have meaning in the context of a belief in a transcendental power, than a matter of crossing boundaries established by a particular culture or society. It just happens that in 18th-century France these boundaries were entirely religious in character.

Whether or not motivated by components of a personal psychology, then, Sade's atheism is not a wholly negative force. It is, first and foremost, a resistance to all political and social constraints.

> Sade against God is Sade against absolute monarchy, Sade against Robespierre, Sade against Napoleon, it is Sade against anything that constitutes any degree or kind of restraint on the shining light of man's subjectivity.
>
> (Gilbert Lely, *Sade*, 1967)

It also represents a liberation that is not only political and moral, but also and above all intellectual. Sade is the only atheistic philosopher of his time to have a physical awareness of the infinite. Sade's awareness of an infinity that is not spiritual but material, a concept which since Einstein we know to be a proven scientific reality, also helps to make him one of the first philosophers of the modern age.

Chapter 4
Sade and the French Revolution

Monarchist or republican?

'What am I?' Sade wrote in 1791 to his lawyer, Gaufridy, 'aristocrat or democrat? Please tell me . . . because I know nothing any more.' This seemingly heartfelt plea suggests a genuine sense of confusion on the part of the now former marquis and citizen of the new French republic, although it has to be said that he was writing to a man whom he knew to be a monarchist. Whichever response to Sade's own question the reader may favour, there are plenty of arguments to be marshalled in support.

Many have accused Sade of unabashed political opportunism in the Revolution. After all, throughout his life, Sade was capable of behaving like any other feudal lord of the manor, pulling rank when it suited him. Moreover, Sade's tendencies towards self-dramatization are never too far below the surface, and the theatre of revolution certainly provided him with ample opportunities to role-play. Indeed, days before the Bastille was stormed, Sade is said to have harangued the street crowds from his cell, urging them to rise up and revolt – perhaps the most theatrical of all episodes in his very theatrical life. Sade consciously dramatized this event, turning it into a founding moment of the French Revolution for the sake of the Revolutionary Tribunal, casting himself in the lead role of 'liberator' of the Bastille. Later,

8. The Bastille

the chance to deliver rousing speeches before appreciative
revolutionary gatherings would have proved especially attractive to
the rhetorician and thespian deprived for so long of theatrical
activity and an adoring public. On the other hand, as Sade's most
recent biographer Neil Shaeffer observes, there was no hypocrisy in
these performances, part of his charm being that, at the time, 'he
truly felt and truly was what he seemed to be'. And of course, Sade
had no love for a monarchy that had kept him in prison without
trial for more than thirteen years, and he was certainly carried
away by the fast pace of events during the revolutionary period.
Moreover, the view that his overtly pro-republican activities at this
time were dictated by pure expediency is hard to credit, when one
might have expected him to adopt a more discreet profile in view of
his aristocratic past.

In the end, Sade's tendency to role-play makes it hard to determine
his true political views on specific issues, and virtually impossible to
pin a political label on him that would assign him a neat place in

9. Man Ray, *Imaginary Portrait of the Marquis de Sade*, 1938

history, though this has not deterred many from trying. We shall return to this question in the conclusion to this chapter.

Another source of confusion in this area is Sade's fictional works. The mistake is often made of conflating Sade's own views with those of his fictional characters. In particular, the political pamphlet

'Frenchmen, one more effort if you wish to be Republicans',
intercalated into *Philosophy in the Boudoir*, is assumed by some
critics to be the unmodulated expression of the author's own
political views. We shall see presently that such a reading is
problematic, to say the least, given the work's parodic and satirical
status, as are readings of political dissertations in *Juliette* (those of
the arch-libertine Noirceuil, for instance) that take them to be the
literal and direct expression of an authorial voice. There is also the
violence of Sade's fictional world, which tempts some readers to
draw dubious analogies with modern political scenarios. This is
exactly what Pier Paolo Pasolini does in his 1975 film *Salò*, in which
Sade's *The 120 Days of Sodom* is used as the model for fascist
atrocities. While Pasolini's film is undoubtedly a work of
considerable artistic merit, it has little to do with the work that
inspired it, and there is a danger that such adaptations invite
audiences to dehistoricize Sade's text, forcing it into an entirely
inappropriate context of modern political thinking. Those who
have attempted to enlist Sade in the ideological vanguard of
'good' (Marxist) or 'evil' (fascist) political movements of later
times are guilty of anachronism and misreading. Taking quite
the opposite tack, some scholars have identified a denial of the
political itself in the isolation that Sade considers fundamental
to the human condition. Far from embracing a particular
political credo, the Sadean text consistently exposes politics
as a corrupt and empty rhetoric, a means of manipulating the
masses. Sade has no optimism about social progress. Indeed,
he has no systematic faith in the need for society at all.
Individuals must be treated according to their individual
make-up, which means that laws that cater for the collective are
redundant.

Sade's attitude to the political is, then, deeply cynical, and his total
lack of belief in historical progress surprisingly pessimistic –
surprising because throughout his life Sade exhibited a great
interest in history. His library in both the Bastille and in Charenton
contained many historical studies, especially on the Middle Ages,

Sade's anti-politics

Needless to say, we had it printed in the press that such were the frightful abuses the government was perpetrating, and that so long as the royal regime prevailed over the Senate and the law, no fortune would be in safety, no citizen would walk in peace abroad or breathe in peace at home. The people believed what they read and sighed for a revolution. Aye, so it is the poor fools are hoodwinked, so it is the common population is at once made the pretext and the victim of its leaders' wickedness: always weak and always stupid, sometimes it is made to want a king, sometimes a republic, and the prosperity its agitators offer under the one system or the other is never but the phantom created by their interests or by their passions.

(*Juliette*, p. 870)

and he himself wrote two historical novels set in that period (*Adélaïde de Brunswick* and *Isabelle de Bavière*). Yet, despite his obvious fascination with the historical process, human history seemed to Sade to be utterly nonsensical and any concept of progress wholly unsupported by the evidence.

Revolutionary pamphlets

Despite the political cynicism expressed in Sade's fictional works of the time, it is undeniable that Sade threw himself into the French Revolution with an enthusiasm astonishing for one with no belief in human progress, fast becoming one of the rising stars of his local section in Paris. This was the Section des Piques, one of the most radical of all the revolutionary sections and of which Robespierre himself was a member. Sade's appointment as a magistrate in April

1793 and his promotion to president of the section by July of that year were in part due to the success of a handful of political essays and speeches. These writings reveal Sade's exceptional rhetorical gifts, but rhetoric and truth do not always coincide. They also provided the consummate actor in Sade with rare opportunities to perform before large and appreciative audiences.

The most important of these essays are the 'On the Method for Approving Laws' of 1792 and the 'Memorial Speech for Marat and Le Peletier' of the following year. Initially delivered as speeches to the Section des Piques, both were highly acclaimed and ordered to be printed and circulated among all the other revolutionary sections.

The first of these essays concerns the passing of laws in the new republic and is strikingly democratic in spirit. Sade proposes that all new laws should be put to the people themselves in their cantonal meetings before being ratified. Rejecting any delegation of power as open to abuse, Sade's argument is that 'Sovereignty is one, indivisible, inalienable, you destroy it by sharing it, you lose it by conferring it on others.' The former marquis expresses here the most radical of republican ideas, commonly associated with Jacobinism and the '*sans-culottes*', the most extreme of all revolutionary factions.

> You now ask which is the best method for sanctioning laws whilst retaining the sovereignty which you have received from nature, which despotism stole from you, and which you have just regained at the cost of your blood? This is what I propose as the quickest and most majestic means of giving the people that indispensable power of sanction without which there is no law for a free nation.
>
> An initial letter will give notice to the mayors of the chief town of each canton of the French territory. As soon as they have received this, they will convene primary assemblies which will meet in the

A parody of Marat?

Scevolus, Brutus, your only merit was to arm yourselves for one moment to end the existence of two despots; your patriotism shone for one hour at most. But you, Marat, by what more difficult road did you lead the life of a free man; how many thorns lay in your path as you pursued your goal; it was among tyrants that you spoke to us of liberty; you adored this goddess whilst we were still ignorant of her sacred name; Machiavelli's daggers hovered above your head from all quarters but your august brow remained unruffled. Scevolus and Brutus each threatened a single tyrant; but your far greater spirit desired the death of all those that overburdened the earth, and slaves accused you of liking blood! Great man, it was theirs that you wished to spill; you were prodigal with their blood, only in order to spare that of the people. With so many enemies, how could you not succumb? While you singled out traitors, you were to be struck down by treachery.

('Memorial Speech for Marat and Le Peletier')

chief town of the canton. Following the wise precautions of our legislators, the proposed law will only then be sent to them in a second mailing. These magistrates of the people will read out the bill to the assembled people. Having been examined, discussed, and carefully studied by the collective mass of individuals that it will serve, this bill will then be accepted or rejected. In the former case, the messenger who has just brought it will immediately take it back, the will of the majority prevailing, and the bill will be promulgated. Should it only secure the support of a minority, your députés must immediately modify, suppress or recast it, and if they succeed in improving it, it should be presented a second time to the whole of

France gathered together in the same way in all cantons of the various départements.

('On the Method for Approving Laws'; author's translation)

Of other essays by Sade at this time, the eulogy of Marat also appears to express support for Jacobin extremism. Was his praise of the bloodiest of all French revolutionaries sincerely intended or a subtle parody of extremist rhetoric? Similarly, was his apparent espousal of democracy born of sincerely held convictions, or was it a cynical manoeuvre designed to establish his credentials as a bona fide republican? Critics are divided on these questions. In the end, it is perhaps futile to conjecture when no definitive answers are possible.

One more effort

Apart from these essays, the expression of political views can also be found throughout Sade's fictional oeuvre, but critics have paid special attention to the intercalated pamphlet, provocatively entitled 'Frenchmen, one more effort if you wish to become republicans', read out by Dolmancé in *Philosophy in the Boudoir*.

The Dolmancé pamphlet can be read as a pastiche of the many political and philosophical *libelles*, or underground pamphlets, circulating in the revolutionary period. The freedom of the press, announced in August 1789, had led to a veritable explosion of such publications, which had been heavily censored under the *ancien régime*. It may also be read as an ironic attack on Robespierre's 'virtuous republic', founded on repression and murder. In it, Sade provides the theory implied in the bloody atrocities of the French Revolution.

Philosophy in the Boudoir was begun during Sade's imprisonment at Picpus in 1794, following his arrest during the Terror by Robespierre for political moderation and alleged royalist

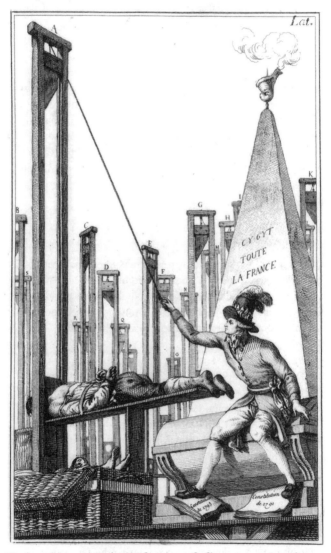

10. Anonymous engraving, 'Robespierre, finding no more executioners, carries out the office himself', 1793

sympathies. From his cell in this former sanatorium, he had a clear view of the guillotine which had been moved to this new location from the Place de la Concorde because of complaints about the smell of blood. The executed were buried in their thousands in the grounds of the sanatorium. Sade watched this bloody slaughter day after day, and declared in correspondence that it affected him greatly. Against the backdrop of these horrific events in Sade's own life, the cruelties of his fictions take on a highly ironic character.

Philosophy in the Boudoir is set some time between July 1794 and October 1795, immediately after the Terror. It is not implausible, therefore, that the intercalated pamphlet was intended as a commentary on topical events. Its central message that vice and, above all, murder are good for a republic is difficult to read as anything but a swingeing satire on the savagery of Robespierre's regime.

And yet, the detailed exposition of a political and sexual philosophy found in the pamphlet is full of contradictions. On the one hand, it appears to support the Revolution in denouncing 'that cast, so justly despised, of royalists and aristocrats', and yet on the other, it indicts the ten members of the Committee of Public Safety for inflicting the

The Terror

This was the bloodiest period of the Revolution, covering about fifteen months, from March 1793 to July 1794. From the beginning of this period up to 10 June 1794, 1,251 persons were executed in Paris. From 10 June to 27 July, there were 1,376 victims. The Committee of Public Safety, with Robespierre at its head, was largely responsible for ordering these executions. The Terror came to an end with the fall and execution of Robespierre on 28 July 1794.

Terror on the French people from the early 1790s, and in so doing committing acts of violence rivalling any cruelties perpetrated by the *ancien régime*. Robespierre is also roundly condemned as the 'priest of religion'. On 7 May 1794, Robespierre had declared the Republic to be Deist and atheism as 'anti-republican'. Written shortly after this date, the pamphlet voices Sade's contempt for this decree. The deism of 'l'infâme Robespierre' and even of Voltaire (a writer much admired by Sade) must be swept away, the pamphlet argues, to be replaced by the paganism of ancient Rome. Since the monarchy and the church are mutually supportive, the church must be stripped of its power. Since history teaches that religion has always served the interests of tyrants, atheism is that 'one more effort' needed for France to become truly republican.

Sade's attack on Robespierre and religion caught the mood of the times, for only a few months later, the architect of the Terror was executed and the cult of the Supreme Being which he had promoted died with him.

The individual and the state

The pamphlet is certainly a polemic, then, but we must not forget that its author is not Sade but an anonymous, fictional scribbler, perhaps Dolmancé himself. As such, we cannot necessarily assume everything in it to be the true opinions of the author, whose motivations in writing it were no doubt many and varied. The overwritten passages expressing patriotic republicanism, for example, are far too sycophantic to be sincere.

By the same token, the pamphlet's advocacy of the rule of law and the 'social principles' of charity, heroism, humanity, and civic spirit read like hollow sentiments when juxtaposed with the presentation in the second part of the pamphlet of a morality rooted solely in self-interest. This section is subtitled '*Les moeurs*', meaning 'morals' but also 'manners' or 'customs'. While sexual morality is the underlying thread, it binds together every major aspect of the functioning of a republican state, from its laws, systems of education, and communication, to the rights and responsibilities of individual citizens. In other words, every feature of the new republic in Sade's Utopian vision of it is seen in terms of sex and individual freedom. This conjunction of sex and politics in relation to the individual is one of the most original features of Sade's thought. A number of 20th-century feminists would succinctly express this idea, according to which there is no divorce between the individual and the public sphere, in a phrase that has now become a commonplace: 'the personal is political'.

To ensure this personal freedom, there must be fewer laws in society. In any case, as no sexual activity can be considered criminal since all morality is relative, not universal, there will be less need for the state to punish. Here, Sade points obliquely to the hypocrisies and excesses of the current regime, and in particular exposes the regime's tendency to overlegislate: between 1789 and 1794, no fewer than 3,400 new laws had been passed. It is the legislators themselves, Sade wryly suggests, who create crimes for there is none in nature. In his championing of the individual at the expense of the state, Sade produces a caricature of Thermidorean discourse. We should also remember that, given his experiences of the courts under the *ancien régime*, Sade had his own reasons to view the law and lawyers with cynicism and contempt.

Whereas this discourse privileged liberty above all things, Sade pushes this liberty to its logical and intolerable extreme, arguing for the freedom to rape and to kill. The irony of this ingenuous-sounding defence of anarchy and violence would not have been lost on the contemporary reader. With monarch and deity gone, the pamphlet continues, only four possible crimes remain: calumny, theft, impurity, and murder, all offences against our fellow-men under the monarchy but none of them serious under a republic! The pamphlet dismisses each of these 'crimes' in tones of understated sarcasm. First, calumny:

The Thermidoreans

Named after the month in the revolutionary calendar when they seized power (July 1794), the counter-revolutionary Thermidoreans put an end to Robespierre's regime of Terror in an even more terrible fashion: 71 men were guillotined in a single day, the biggest bloodbath of the entire Revolution. In doing so, they also put an end to the Revolution itself. Yet, the Thermidoreans were in no way admirable, motivated principally by self-preservation. It was more than a year before they attempted to provide the new republic with a constitution, and in doing so were torn between their fear of both democracy and dictatorship. The draft that emerged consequently proposed a limited franchise giving power to the propertied classes alone. These proposals eventually led to a popular rising in Paris on 5 October 1795. Although this revolt was brutally put down, the event marked the end of the Thermidorean period, and the advent of the Directory, new rulers drawn from a new class of *nouveaux riches*.

It is with utmost candour I confess that I have never considered calumny an evil, and especially in a government like our own, under which all of us, bound closer together, nearer one to the other, obviously have a greater interest in becoming acquainted with one another.

(pp. 311–12)

Given the internecine divisions of the revolutionary period, this can be read as a devastating attack on the ideal of republican brotherhood. In an earlier scene in the main dialogue, Dolmancé had put things rather more directly:

are we not all born solitary, isolated? [. . .] are we not come into the world all enemies, the one of the other, all in a state of perpetual and reciprocal warfare?

(pp. 283–4)

Theft is perfectly justified since wealth is so unfairly distributed in society – a sentiment scathingly critical of the corruption of the revolutionary years, and, for the modern reader, Marxist *avant la lettre*. As for the 'impure crimes' of prostitution, adultery, incest, rape, and sodomy, how can individuals be expected to behave in a morally correct fashion when the state clearly behaves immorally by conducting wars?

The pamphlet reserves its most biting irony, however, for the 'offence' of murder, the very cornerstone of the Revolution itself:

> Is [murder] a political crime? We must avow, on the contrary, that it is, unhappily, merely one of policy's and politics' greatest instruments. Is it not by dint of murders that France is free today?
>
> (p. 332)

Watching victim upon victim climb the steps to the guillotine from his cell at Picpus and breathing in the stench of blood as he wrote such lines, it is inconceivable that Sade really intended such a lack of regard for human life to be taken seriously.

Juliette

Detailed expositions of views similar to those expressed in 'Frenchmen, one more effort' can be found especially in *Juliette*, where a direct satirical purpose is not always so easy to discern, and where the contradictions are therefore far more blatant.

In *Juliette*, the eponymous heroine meets up with some of the leading political figures in Europe before the Revolution: Catherine the Great, Gustavus of Sweden, Pope Pius VI, Ferdinand of Naples,

Victor-Amédée of Savoy, and Leopold of Tuscany. All of these monarchs are attacked by Juliette, who tells the Pope, for example, that revolutionary change will soon sweep over the whole of Europe. Writing in the 1790s with the hindsight of history, Sade is not averse to pandering to his reader's spirit of revolution and loathing of the French monarchy. Sade's portrayal of the debauchery of Europe's monarchs and princes echoes the lubricious content of those pornographic pamphlets aimed at the French King and Queen that played such a crucial role in preparing the ground for revolution in France. Such pamphlets had circulated throughout the 1780s, mocking Louis XVI's alleged impotence, and accusing Marie-Antoinette of indulging in depraved sexual orgies with her courtiers.

In contrast, there may appear to be numerous counter-revolutionary notes in *Juliette*. All of the libertines praise despotism and terror, some even demanding a return to feudalism. We should remember, however, that it is, precisely, the villainous characters of the novel who express such views, and that they are not to be simplistically equated with those of the author. Sade's own voice is always cloaked in irony, and if we read carefully between the lines, it is not hard to discern a far more subtle politics than that of his libertine anti-heroes. When it is pointed out to the libertine Borchamps that he is himself a tyrant, and yet he detests tyranny, the libertine's response is a telling piece of cynicism and ambiguity:

> If the Senate is ready to rise in arms against Sweden's sovereign, it is not from horror of tyranny but from envy at seeing despotism exercised by another than itself [...] *the throne is to everybody's taste, and 'tis not the throne they detest, but him who is seated on it.*
> (*Juliette*, pp. 861–2)

Is Sade to be regarded, then, as more of a feudal aristocrat at heart than a true revolutionary? We may have to accept that Sade can be either at different times and in different contexts, as it suits him, and that, in the end, no single reading of Sade's politics is wholly satisfactory.

After examining his works, one is left with the impression that Sade's chameleon character is, in the political as in so many other domains, ultimately undecidable, which, in an odd way, is more subversive than any fixed political position would be. The ambiguity of both the content of Sade's declarations on politics, as well as the ambiguity of their tone (serious or ironic?), undermines any aim of political alignment, casting doubt on the plausibility, or indeed the desirability, of a polarized set of views. On the one hand, Sade's ambiguous political relativism might be seen as wholly in tune with the increasing moral scepticism of the late Enlightenment, while, on the other, Sade expresses the political cynicism towards the *ancien régime* that was prevalent in the revolutionary period, and most strikingly of all, perhaps, perfectly captures the lure of absolute power that infected political leaders throughout the 1790s, and that culminated in the establishment of a dictatorship by Napoleon in 1799. In this sense, Sade offers his readers an accurate and not uncritical reflection of the unstable political situation in France at the end of the 18th century.

Chapter 5
Theatres of the body

All the world's a stage

Throughout his adult life, Sade devoted himself energetically to the putting on of plays, frequently assuming leading roles himself in his productions. The appeal of a physical medium well suited to Sade's sensual and extrovert personality may offer some explanation for his fascination with theatre. It is hardly surprising, therefore, that Sade should have written a significant corpus of more than twenty plays himself, including examples of all the principal genres of 18th-century theatre (comedy, drama, melodrama, and tragedy). Yet, partly perhaps because they were not available to the public until 1970, there has been little critical interest in the plays. There is some irony in this, since, like Voltaire before him, Sade valued his dramatic writing above all else, and yet, as with Voltaire, Sade is remembered for his novels, not his theatre. Only those few plays composed by Sade during the revolutionary period that served republican propaganda in denouncing the libertinage of the aristocracy ever reached the public stage. Although the plays contain no explicit obscenity, even those that did reach the stage such as *Count Oxtiern, or the Effects of Libertinism*, were considered to have controversial themes. The majority of them were composed in prison between 1780 and 1789, alongside the major novels, and share their preoccupation with incest, adultery, rape, and murder. However, the plays were purely conventional in style, and overall contributed nothing really new to the genre.

Sade continued to write plays after the Revolution, during the 1790s, and also in the asylum at Charenton, where he staged his own and other works. In spite of his relative failure as a playwright, Sade's attachment to the theatre was, then, profound and enduring. An outlet for his exhibitionist tendencies, the dramatic is also the ideal medium for the representation of the sexual, and while the sexed body could not be openly represented on the 18th-century stage, there was still the virtual stage of Sade's prose works, all of which, whether novels, essays, or even letters and diaries, exhibit a fundamental theatricality. Paradoxically, it is not in the plays but in these prose writings that Sade's dramatic gifts are most effectively exploited, and among these *The 120 Days of Sodom* and *Philosophy in the Boudoir* use the vehicle of theatre in the most striking and the most original fashion.

Both *The 120 Days* and *Boudoir* are essentially theatrical works in which the naked body of ancient Greek comedy is taken one logical and outrageous step further: in Sade's theatre, the body is not just a sexed body, or even a body that counterfeits sex for satirical purposes, as in the plays of Aristophanes. At a time when the conventional theatre of his day was becoming increasingly abstract, Sade took his 'libertine theatre' as far in the opposite direction as it was possible to imagine, to construct the first sex-shows of the modern era. Sade's 'scripts' for the performance of real sexual acts have little in common, however, with the mindless pornographic spectacles of Pigalle, Amsterdam, or Soho one can pay to see today. Uniquely in the history of modern drama, Sade's theatres of the body demonstrate in disturbing yet compelling fashion the fundamental interrelatedness of sex and philosophy.

The 120 Days of Sodom

Though not strictly dramatic in format, *The 120 Days of Sodom* is in every other sense theatrical, from its melodramatic setting to the very manner in which it is constructed. In this startlingly novel work, Sade represents the body as spectacle, but he also dramatizes the very process of narration itself.

The circumstances surrounding the composition and eventual loss of *The 120 Days* were themselves the very stuff of drama. Sade began it in prison on 22 October 1785, writing in microscopic handwriting on long, narrow rolls of paper which he glued together into a roll that was eventually 49 feet long, kept hidden in a hole in the wall of his cell in the Bastille. In the ironically named Tower of Liberty where his cell was located, he wrote every evening after dinner for three hours or more, taking only 37 days to produce a novel-length draft of the first of four sections and detailed notes for the remaining three. It is not known precisely why Sade abandoned the manuscript at this point, since it was clearly incomplete. Perhaps he became preoccupied with other writings: for example, his long philosophical novel, *Aline and Valcour*, many short stories, including the first version of the *Justine* narrative, 'The Misfortunes of Virtue', and a number of plays were all composed over the next few years. Then, ten days before the storming of the Bastille in 1789, Sade was moved without warning to another fortress, and although his wife had already managed to smuggle finished work out of the Bastille, he had no opportunity to take any unfinished work with him. To his great chagrin, therefore, he never saw *The 120 Days* again. Eventually, the manuscript was discovered and remained in private hands until the early 20th century when the German psychiatrist Dr Iwan Bloch, under the pseudonym Eugen Dühren, published a first limited edition of the work. Maurice Heine acquired the manuscript on behalf of Viscount Charles de Noailles in 1929, and provided a much revised version in the early 1930s. Both of these early editions were produced for the benefit of doctors and scientists working in the new field of sexology. Sade's

11. *The 120 Days of Sodom manuscript*

extraordinary work had acquired a reputation in these circles as the first known encyclopedia of sexual aberrations, foreshadowing the theories of Krafft-Ebing and Freud by more than a century. The work was considered to be an important scientific resource for anyone studying the classification of human sexuality.

In the narrower context of Sade's writing as a whole, the *120 Days* may be regarded as the corner-stone of the Sadean edifice, containing a number of features that would become characteristic of his novel-writing: an obsession with order, categorization, and numbers; a narrative pattern based on the alternation of dissertation and orgy (or of theory and practice); and, above all, a mission, unique in literature, to describe, catalogue, and illustrate all possible manifestations of human sexuality.

The work is set in the first decade of the 18th century during the last years of the reign of Louis XIV. The novel's four libertine protagonists use the huge profits they have made from Louis' military campaigns to indulge in a four-month-long orgy of depravity, rape, and murder. The events of these four months are assigned to four separate parts, but Part 1 alone was completed. The violence increases in intensity and horror from month to month, criminal and murderous passions being reserved for the third and fourth months respectively. However, there is very little violence in the completed Part 1, while the violence of the remaining sections is outlined so schematically as to remain somewhat abstract. The most sadistic of acts are merely listed in Parts 3 and 4 almost without commentary and in a deadpan, emotionless style.

The orgies take place in a remote castle, the Château de Silling, owned by one of the four libertines, perched on a high peak in the depths of the Black Forest. The narrator emphasizes Silling's total inaccessibility, 'a remote and isolated retreat, as if silence, distance, and stillness were libertinage's potent vehicles' (p. 235), a fastness that offers the four criminals the freedom to do whatever they wish with complete impunity, while denying any hope of escape or rescue to their unfortunate victims. This remoteness is consolidated when a huge quantity of snow falls in the surrounding valley, strengthening the castle's isolation, and smothering the cries of both torturer and victim. The libertines are thus completely cut off from the outside world for the four winter months of their protracted orgy. Affording the libertines virtually unlimited power, this geographical location could not have been more different from the constrained circumstances in which Sade was writing in his prison cell in the Bastille, and it seems plausible to conjecture that on one level, he was creating an imaginary libertine Utopia to make up for the real physical freedoms he had lost.

Indeed, the Château de Silling is strongly reminiscent of the prisons of Vincennes and the Bastille itself where the work was composed, though there are also echoes of the various provençal castles owned by the Sade family, especially La Coste and Saumane where the young Sade had spent much of his childhood. In fact, some maintain that Silling is identical in construction to the La Coste château, where he was known to have conducted a number of real-life orgies, although there is no evidence that any of these involved the extreme violence and murder depicted in the fiction.

The four main actors of the piece represent the four sources of authority and power in 18th-century France (the nobility, the church, the courts, and high finance), and their largely negative portrayal further suggests that the work is intended to be read on one level as political satire. All four protagonists are represented at the outset both in terms of their unmitigated abuse of wealth and power and their sexual manias, suggesting a direct link between them. Significantly, three of the four are depicted as sexually inadequate, implying a further link between the kind of sexual frustration experienced by the imprisoned author and the potential for violence towards others. The leader of the group, the 50-year-old Duke de Blangis, is painted as an unscrupulous and cowardly sex-fiend who has already killed his mother, sister, and three of his wives, and whose sexual aberration is excess rather than inadequacy: permanently priapic, his ejaculations have the character of violent epileptic fits. His brother, a bishop, aged 45, has murdered two young children for their money. Unlike Blangis, whose penis is 12 inches long by 8 inches in circumference, the Bishop has a 'very ordinary, even little' member, a measure of the contempt in which Sade held the Catholic clergy. The 53-year-old financier, Durcet, also has an 'extraordinarily small' penis and the breasts and buttocks of a woman to boot. Like Durcet, who poisoned his mother, his wife, and his niece in order to inherit their wealth, the Président du Curval, a physically repulsive magistrate of 60, owes his fortune to debauchery and murder. While the Bishop and Durcet suffer from inadequately sized penises, Curval has difficulty achieving erection, although, when they do occur, his orgasms are as explosive as Blangis's. Sade himself experienced problems ejaculating, and yet, like Blangis, his orgasms had the force of volcanic eruptions. These sexual idiosyncrasies are reflected in the sexual portraits of his four protagonists, which represent the two extremes of virtual impotence (Curval) and unlimited potency (Blangis).

The notes for sections 2–4 depict the lusts and perversions of bankers, lawyers, magistrates, priests, courtiers, landowners, military officers, all old, rich, powerful, and just as repulsive as the four main protagonists. All these figures represent the ruling classes of the *ancien régime*, whom Sade despised for the part they had played in his downfall. In this early work, composed under what the author experienced as the tyranny of a corrupt and degenerate monarchy, libertinage is certainly not painted in attractive hues, in contrast to those libertine novels Sade would write after the Revolution.

As in all of Sade's writings, sodomy and incest are foregrounded, all four libertines taking pleasure in activities which both church and state regarded in the 18th century as unnatural and criminal offences. While the Duke alone enjoys vaginal penetration, he shares the preference of the other three for sodomy with his own sex. Despite this, each of the three debauchees has married the daughter of one of the others, in a perverse parody of the bourgeois patriarchal system of marriage, according to which fathers marry off their daughters to the sons of other wealthy men in order to obtain property and other financial interests. As the Bishop cannot marry, and therefore cannot participate properly in the system of exchange, his daughter is regarded as common sexual property by the others. Blangis, Curval, and Durcet all have sex with their own daughters, while exchanging them with the other two as a means of strengthening their common alliance. Sade thus simultaneously undermines the family structure and the incest taboo.

These daughter-wives share their victim status with a harem of twenty-eight others: sixteen young boys and girls aged between 12 and 15, all beautiful virgins; eight 'studs' in their 20s, chosen for the impressive size of their penis and their sexual potency; and four repulsive and depraved old women. Dressed in costumes that accentuate their sexual availability, the delicious young virgins form a marked contrast with the old hags, a contrast the libertines find highly arousing.

Four story-tellers, three cooks, and three kitchen servants make up the rest of the château's residents. As the source of all the food and alcohol consumed, the cooks enjoy a special status, which insures them against all harm. So too do the story-tellers, who occupy centre-stage throughout: Duclos, Champville, Martaine, and Desgranges are all prostitutes of many years' experience. Their function is to narrate in meticulous detail tales of sexual perversion that will subsequently be re-enacted by the listening libertines. The story-tellers effectively dramatize the very process of narration, illustrating the power of language to excite and taking the physicality of theatre to its logical extreme in transforming the body itself into principal actor.

This theatricality informs the spaces of the novel. In addition to the melodramatic nature of the castle setting and location, the

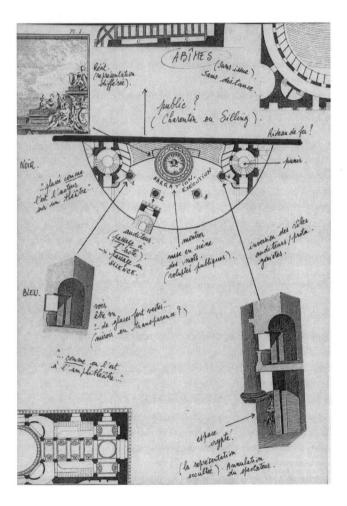

12. Daniele Bello, imaginary drawings for the theatre of *The 120 Days of Sodom*

narration of stories and the communal orgiastic activities that these stories are intended to promote take place in a main hall, designed in the semi-circular shape of an amphitheatre. Each story-teller sits on a centrally positioned throne when her turn comes to narrate, while the four libertines occupy seats in four separate recesses. Like extras waiting in the wings, the victims sit on steps below the throne and within easy reach of the four libertines in their respective recesses. On either side of the throne stands a column to which victims can be attached and on which hang instruments of 'correction' and torture. Closets lead off from each recess, providing the individual libertine with a space for activities which he would rather conduct in private. The main space is, nevertheless, both public and dramatic. Resembling theatre in the round, this space is designed so that the libertines can see and hear all that occurs in every corner, in the other recesses as much as in the throne area. Debauchery here is above all a shared dramatic experience, in which it is as important to be seen as to see. Acting out their own desire, the four protagonists are also audience to that of others. What is staged at Silling, in this theatre that is so emphatically cut off from the real world, is the unreality of desire, but also its very *mise en scène*, or representation, as narration itself becomes the dominant subject of the work.

The story-tellers hold the stage for most of the time, relating episodes experienced or witnessed by them that illustrate the 600 perversions, or 'passions', to be covered, and provoking the libertines to act out what they have heard. The four listening friends effectively substitute for the male reader, showing him what to do.These tales depict some of the most appalling activities found in Sade's fictions, including coprophilia and, in the final part of the book, horrific torture and murder of the most sadistic kind imaginable. The four libertines respond by inflicting similar atrocities on their captives. The eating of faeces, for instance, becomes a ritualistic event required of victims and enjoyed by the libertines.

13. Jacques Bioulès, model of the assembly hall of the Château of Silling, 1989

As the months pass, victims are selected to be abused, and finally killed, in gruesome fashion. For example, the 15-year-old Augustine is whipped, sodomized, boiling oil poured into her wounds, a red-hot poker thrust into her vagina and anus. She undergoes many more horrible tortures before dying, including the laying bare of the nerves in her body which are then scraped with a knife. The horror of scenes such as this is to some degree attenuated by the fantastical nature of the acts to which victims like Augustine are subjected; so theoretical, one might say, as to invite a symbolic or psychoanalytic, rather than a realist, reading:

> [. . .] a hole is bored in her throat, her tongue is drawn back, down, and passed through it, 'tis a comical effect, they broil her remaining breast, then, clutching a scalpel, the Duc thrusts his hand into her cunt and cuts through the partition dividing the anus from the vagina; he throws aside the scalpel, reintroduces his hand, and

70

rummaging about in her entrails, forces her to shit through her
cunt [. . .]

(pp. 658–9)

The grim humour of such descriptions has a similarly de-realizing
effect.

In all of these scenarios, whether narrated or enacted, it is the very
idea of transgression, of the breaking of taboos, that the libertine
finds erotic, rather than the act itself:

'it is not the object of libertine intentions which fires us', says
Blangis, 'but the idea of evil, and [. . .] consequently it is thanks only
to evil and only in the name of evil one stiffens, not thanks to the
object.'

(p. 364)

The reader is further distanced from the text by not being addressed
directly, except in the Introduction, in addition to being distanced
from the action narrated in that text by the story-telling situation.
This distancing inevitably has the effect of diminishing both the
erotic and the horrific impact on the reader, as does the work's
pedagogical character (its subtitle is 'The School of Libertinage').
Furthermore, these 'embedded' narratives are framed by the
author's controlling narration which, far from seeking to arouse
the reader located outside the text, contains frequent references
to the narrative process within it. There are many lists of characters,
of errors the author intends to correct, and there are warnings to
the reader of what is to come, and instructions on how to use the
work, in the manner of a foreword to a school textbook. These
references and authorial interruptions also help to de-realize
and de-eroticize the text, moving the focus away from sexual
desire and sadistic cruelty to the process of writing and
discourse. In fact, *The 120 Days* functions inefficiently as a
work of pornography, since the reader's interest is constantly
displaced from any erotic effect to the ways in which sexuality is

71

represented through linguistic, arithmetical, and other formal structures.

The transparency of these structures may be seen as both positive and negative. There is certainly an obsession with form running throughout the narrative that wears the patience of the most assiduous of readers. On the other hand, this focus draws attention away from the horror of the content, and it also generates some strongly innovative features: a reader-centredness created by the many references to the reading process; the performativity of narration, the staging of the pornographic effect, as words and images are seen to give rise to acts. Such features are all of undeniable interest in the context of both critical theory and the current debate concerning the influence of pornography. A self-consciously dramatic representation of the pornographic process rather than an instance of pornography itself, *The 120 Days of Sodom* will provide an important template for the libertine works to come.

Philosophy in the Boudoir

Unlike *The 120 Days*, *Philosophy in the Boudoir* has an explicitly dramatic form. This does not of course mean that the work was intended for performance – it is hard to see how it could ever have reached a public stage in the 18th century – but its dialogic structure does at least indicate that it was intended to be read *as theatre*, to be performed in the mind's eye. And as in *The 120 Days*, it is the sexed body that takes centre-stage.

Published in 1795, shortly after Sade's release from prison, this cheerfully obscene work is more memorable for its physical and verbal comedy than for its rare moments of violence and cruelty. One of Sade's most complex works, *Boudoir* can be read on a number of levels: as well as dramatic dialogue, it is also a philosophical and political polemic, a literary parody, and a Chaucerian farce.

But like *The 120 Days*, *Boudoir*'s main impact has always been as a particularly scandalous form of sexual pedagogy, and in this case, Sade was almost certainly influenced by earlier models (Michel Millot's and Jean l'Ange's *L'École des filles* of 1688, and Nicolas Chorier's *L'Académie des dames* of about 1660).

Sade's text innovates, however, in taking the reader into a specifically feminine space, the boudoir of the title (mistranslated in some English editions as 'bedroom'), meaning an elegant salon into which ladies can retire. In libertine literature, the boudoir is more narrowly associated with sexual flirting. The title itself, then, seems to sum up the whole Sadean project, which is to bring the body, and in particular the female body, back into philosophy. The work's subtitle, 'or the immoral teachers', explicitly acknowledges its immoral content. Both title and subtitle, then, encapsulate the two dominant impulses in Sade: the intellectual (philosophy, teachers) and the erotic (boudoir, immoral), the mind and the body, underlining the work's status as both sexual instruction and transgressive pornography.

The actors of this obscene theatre are all young and physically desirable. Dolmancé, an active and passive sodomite, described as 'the most profound seducer, the most corrupt, the most dangerous man' (p. 191), is 36, while the other libertines are all under 30. Eugénie, whose sexual initiation is the pretext for the party, is a young virgin of 15. Her father, himself a well-known libertine and one of the richest merchants of Paris, has given permission for all that both daughter and mother are to undergo. The bisexual Mme de Saint-Ange, who will play a leading role in Eugénie's debauchery, is 26. Her brother, the Chevalier de Mirval, is at 20 the youngest of the libertines, a sexual athlete with an extraordinarily large penis: 'Oh, dearest friend,' cries Eugénie on seeing it for the first time, 'what a monstrous member! . . . I can scarcely get my hand around it!' (p. 261). He prefers women, but can be persuaded to engage in sodomy with 'an agreeable man' like Dolmancé. Eugénie's mother, the devout Mme de Mistival, is 32 'at the most', her beauty undimmed. In addition to these five principals, there are two minor characters: Augustin, a young gardener of 'about eighteen or twenty', who is even more impressively endowed than the Chevalier; and Lapierre, Dolmancé's similarly well-equipped but syphilitic valet.

The paradise of the body

These seven actors will re-enact Christianity's founding myth of Genesis in the course of seven 'dialogues', or scenes, inverting its central message, as the Eve-like Eugénie's rejection of God and her passage from sexual innocence to sexual knowledge are celebrated rather than lamented. As we shall see, it is the pious mother, not the sacrilegious and debauched daughter, who is finally expelled from this perverse paradise of the body. Like the biblical Eden, their boudoir is a 'delightful' space, a privileged and almost timeless realm isolated from the outside world, but unlike the Christian version, the delights it affords are physical, not spiritual. There is no original sin in Sade's sexual Utopia: unlike Adam and Eve, Eugénie and her mentors are not only unashamed in their nudity but consider it entirely natural. The only serpent is Augustin's delightfully monstrous penis – 'Look sharp, Eugénie,' Dolmancé warns his fascinated pupil as the gardener is about to ejaculate, 'mind, the serpent is about to disgorge its venom' (p. 268).

This nakedness is not merely a state of undress, but a total laying bare of the human body, as Eugénie is given an advanced lesson in male and female anatomy, both external and internal. Though Dolmancé's lesson contains some erroneous, and largely male-centred, notions of female biology – for example, that male sperm are alone responsible for the creation of life – Sade's text here displays a remarkable knowledge of the female body and of female sexual response, and some, though not all, of the views on sexuality that it contains appear strikingly modern. Women can only orgasm through stimulation of the clitoris, Saint-Ange implies when she tells her pupil, 'there lies all a woman's power of sensation' (p. 204), and she expresses pro-abortion sentiments with which many a modern feminist would sympathize: 'we are always mistress of what we carry in our womb' (p. 249). There is enlightened advice on contraceptive methods of the time (contraception, Eugénie is persuaded, is far preferable to abortion): options range from mechanical methods (the use of dildos, sponges, condoms) to natural methods (hand-relief, fellatio, cunnilingus, 'sixty-nine'). Among the latter, masturbation and sodomy, which the 'absurd' doctrines of Christianity have held to be mortal sins, are seen to be especially helpful in avoiding pregnancy. The defence of sodomy as universally practised by both sexes is found throughout Sade's writing, and was subversive on both a political and a religious level at a time when the act was a capital offence. As for masturbation, Eugénie is given accurate and detailed lessons in the best techniques for both men and women that would not be out of place in a modern sex-education manual. Again, Sade's view was startlingly enlightened for a century in which semen loss was widely believed to cause syphilis (which by the 1790s had reached epidemic proportions) and self-abuse directly linked to insanity.

The positive advocacy of both sodomy and masturbation derives from the central theme of Sade's philosophy of sexuality: the enjoyment of sex for its own sake, rather than for the purposes of procreation, a view running counter to the entire Christian tradition, but that Dolmancé claims to be intended by Nature. Does Nature not allow the loss of sperm in all kinds of situations, other than for propagation? If women's sexual function is solely reproductive, why is their reproductive capacity limited to such a relatively short period in their lives? Clearly, argues Dolmancé, it is natural for human beings to have sex for pleasure alone. This view of sex as a source of pleasure, free of guilt and unshackled by the Christian institution of marriage, was especially liberating for women: 'Women are not made for one single man; 'tis for men at large Nature created them' (p. 286), and what men have called the 'crime' of adultery is a natural right.

14. Illustrations for the first known edition of *La Philosophie dans le boudoir*, 1975

Thus, Eugénie is systematically initiated into every conceivable sexual act, including vaginal and anal penetration, fellatio, cunnilingus, and even the fetishistic use of dildos. In addition to the sex lessons, Eugénie is lectured on various aspects of morality. The modern reader will find some logical inconsistency in the arguments supporting the views expressed here, views that are based on what is observed to be the natural law but essentially derive from pragmatic self-interest. For instance, Dolmancé mounts a spirited defence of rape, incest, prostitution, and even murder (for example, of handicapped babies), while the death penalty is declared to be 'barbarous and stupid' because it merely punishes one crime with another.

When Eugénie's sexual and moral education is complete, the party is interrupted by the delivery of a letter from the girl's father, warning of the imminent arrival of her mother on a mission to rescue her wayward daughter. The dénouement of this sexual spectacle thus takes the form of a *coup de théâtre* that ironically inverts the convention of the popular melodrama, according to which virtue is finally triumphant. It is clear from the outset that the devout Mme de Mistival is going to be the victim of the piece. Eugénie herself, rather than her libertine mentors, will officiate at the sacrifice. Dolmancé does initiate the scenario, by sodomizing and whipping Mme de Mistival, and generally directs the proceedings, but, after she has been similarly abused by the others, it is the daughter who, having vaginally penetrated and then sodomized her own mother with a dildo, carries out the final sentence. Dolmancé's syphilitic valet, Lapierre, is ordered to rape and sodomize the hapless victim, so that she will be infected with his pox, and Eugénie enthusiastically agrees to sew up her vagina and anus to prevent the germs from escaping.

Well and truly stitched up, Mme de Mistival is expelled from the privileged space of the boudoir, infected with a disease generally associated with sexual immorality. The daughter's 'original sin' and the death it symbolizes have been transferred to the mother, and the

daughter is at liberty to continue her enjoyment of Sade's paradise
of the body.

Critical interpretations of the 'needlework' scene

This scene has attracted more critical comment than any other in
the work, partly because of the wide range of responses, from
revulsion to amusement, it seems to elicit, but mainly because it
lends itself so easily to metaphorical and symbolic readings,
especially of the psychoanalytic variety. The scene is also an
excellent example of the role and meaning of transgression in Sade's
theatre of eroticism.

This transgressive dimension does not necessarily depend on a
realist interpretation of the scene, whose verbal and physical
comedy, on the contrary, explode its tragic potential. Eugénie's
treatment of her mother would certainly appear utterly repulsive if
taken seriously, but the knockabout comedy and linguistic humour
undermine any attempt to read the scene on a realist level. The
mother is effectively transformed into an object, just as, in some
modern cartoons, living creatures are treated as things and
subjected to all kinds of horrific violence. In both cases, the visual
and verbal humour renders the violence farcical, and the victim
recovers to live another day.

Whilst the mother bemoans her fate in melodramatic yet controlled
language that seems at the least to understate the gravity of her
situation – 'Oh, my God! what a hideous damnation! [. . .] Oh, my
God! the pain! [. . .] Aïe! aïe! aïe! [. . .] Oh pardon me, Monsieur,
I beg your pardon a thousand thousand times over . . . you are
killing me . . . ' (pp. 363–5) – Eugénie keeps missing her aim with
the needle because of the delirious state of pleasure occasioned by
the Chevalier's intimate fondling. Eugénie's irony, as she performs
the unthinkable, only serves further to emphasize the scene's
humorous potential and to deflate the horror – 'Better that than
to die, Mamma; at least I'll be able to wear some gay dresses this

summer' (p. 363) – while the terms in which the mother voices her pain are confusingly similar to Sade's favourite signifier of *jouissance*: 'vous me faites mourir! . . . ' (p. 308), which translates as 'I'm dying (with pleasure)!' Once the joke is performed, the scene, and indeed the narrative, end with Mme de Mistival's unceremonious dismissal. Thus, the victim lives, to recover from an abuse which, though painful and shocking, is, we assume, not irreversible. A humorous response to this and other such scenes of objectification and dehumanization is only possible because the reader is prevented by the very process itself from identifying too closely with 'rounded' individuals and so from reacting sympathetically when these individuals suffer harm.

The sewing-up of orifices occurs also in *The 120 Days* and in *Juliette*, and this repetition of the motif from work to work suggests that it carries unconscious symbolic meanings. In all cases, there is less emphasis on the pain and cruelty associated with the act than with its practical consequences: the prevention of sexual activity and, especially, of procreation, which is regarded with contempt by Sade's libertines; but, more interestingly perhaps, the closing-up of the female body may metaphorically represent an unconscious desire to shut down sex itself, or at the very least to punish all women for their sexual inaccessibility.

The scene can also be read in terms of Freud's theory of the male castration-complex. In a Freudian perspective, Eugénie's sewing-up of her mother's genitals is an unconscious attempt on the part of the male author to cover up the absence of the lost phallus, and so to assuage his fear of castration. Eugénie has already symbolically restored to herself the lost phallus by strapping on the dildo to rape her mother.

In a different psychoanalytic perspective, the novelist Angela Carter sees the mother as a conflation of both parents and, as such, a novel Oedipal object. For Carter, the daughter's action is essentially about freeing herself from maternal control and achieving sexual autonomy. Eugénie is an unconscious persona of the author, who must punish the mother for having brought him into this miserable world. As Carter observes, 'it is the very fact of generation that he finds intolerable', arguing that Eugénie sews her mother up to prevent the arrival of siblings who might compete for nourishment by the 'good breast', a symbol of the satisfaction of basic human needs. The Sadean libertine unconsciously yearns for total isolation, in which his enjoyment of the world is unhampered by the presence of others.

Eugénie's closing-up of her mother's sexual orifices also has the effect of preventing her mother from competing with her sexually at a time when her own orifices have just been opened up. The need to rescue daughters from maternal authority so that they might be sexually free is a recurrent theme in Sade's fiction, and indeed accurately reflects familial relations in the middle and upper classes of 18th-century France, whereby daughters were kept under their mothers' control until marriage. In this sense, the 'needlework' scene is transgressive of social as well as moral and sexual norms.

This liberation of daughter from mother has also been read in terms of transgression of the incest taboo, which for the social anthropologist Claude Lévi-Strauss is necessary for the exchange of women by men in the marital contracts of patriarchal society. Abolition of this taboo therefore liberates women and, in particular, frees girls from their mothers, whose function is essentially to prepare their daughters to become the wives of men outside the family group. The education of daughters, which the epigraph implies will be a dominant aim of the work ('daughters should be instructed to read this by their mothers'), is therefore designed to remove them from the monogamous family system founded on male power, and the exchange of women underpinning it, an exchange that crucially depends on the preservation of the daughters' virginity. It is this system of sexual taboos antithetical to libertinage that Sade symbolically demolishes in the 'needle scene', in which the mother's authority over her daughter is decisively broken and the mother is punished for her role as enforcer of sexual prohibitions.

Sade's choice, on this occasion, of an overtly theatrical medium is well-suited to the ambivalence of his thought, as the absence of a narrator makes it much more difficult to identify an authorial voice or a unified message. The weight of evidence certainly suggests that Dolmancé and Saint-Ange act largely as mouthpieces for the author, and the polemical pamphlet intercalated in the middle of the work has all the characteristics of an authorial polemic, but the explicitly theatrical format (as opposed to the novelistic format of his other major libertine works) more readily accommodates the philosophical dialogue which is Sade's stock-in-trade, facilitating the expression of different viewpoints. This format also, of course, privileges the physical and the visual, and so is far better suited than prose to the practical demonstration that underpins this work's sex-show-style pedagogy: if the message of sexual liberation is to be truly effective, pleasure cannot just be catalogued, it must be staged. But the actors are not the only ones on this textual stage, for alongside Eugénie, the reader too is implicitly invited to join in the debauchery by following the example set by Eugénie and her libertine instructors, and this is an innovation that overturns the classical relationship of the reader with the printed page.

The ironic use of theatrical vocabulary to denote physical pleasure reinforces a notion of the body itself as actor: 'What a fine spectacle!' cries Eugénie, as the Chevalier covers her with semen. In the dramatic context in which it is expressed, the word 'spectacle' is literal and self-reflexive as well as metaphorical. Sade in fact pushes 'theatre as spectacle' to its extreme, exposing the naked body to the gaze of the putative spectator, but taking this gaze beyond mere voyeurism, as we have seen, to a point of saturation; past the surface to the internal organs of reproduction. This has the effect of

82

transforming the body into a banal object, to be examined, prodded, measured, turned upside down, and ultimately rendered familiar rather than strange. The characters arrange themselves into orgiastic chains with the deadpan efficiency and comically incongruous athleticism of circus acrobats. There is also a comic incongruity between the use of a mannered dramatic idiom, on the one hand, and its licentious contents on the other. These features are more characteristic of farce or satire than pornography.

Chapter 6
Representations of the feminine

Justine and *Juliette* are the works for which Sade is best known. They appeared in the 1790s after the Revolution, and in many important respects reflect the historical circumstances in which they were produced (see Chapter 4). Nevertheless, recent critics have tended to focus their attention on the ways in which women are represented in these novels, responses varying widely from downright hostility (Sade is a misogynistic pornographer for whom women are nothing more than sex objects) to unqualified admiration (Juliette is an early role model for the modern liberated woman). Before we look at the detail of the two narratives in order to assess the accuracy of such judgements, a number of general observations can be made.

The overwhelming majority of female characters in these novels are victims of male sexual violence. Of these, Justine is the leading example. In *Juliette*, however, there are a few independent-minded and even powerful women, notably the eponymous heroine herself. The early 20th-century poet Guillaume Apollinaire expressed a vision of Juliette as 'woman reborn', as this 'creature that we cannot yet conceive, but which is freeing itself from humanity, which will take wing and will renew the universe'. As we shall see, Juliette does indeed exhibit characteristics which we would now associate with female liberation. However, other aspects of her portrayal undermine this view, and to hail Sade as a precursor of feminism, as a few have done, is highly problematic.

At the same time, it would be inappropriate to judge this, or any other element of Sade's writing, according to the values and mores of the 21st century. If some aspects of Sade's attitude to the feminine prove misogynistic by our own standards, it has to be said that, in this, he merely reflects the practices and prejudices of his age: 18th-century French society, like that of the rest of Europe, considered women's proper place to be in the home, serving their husbands' interests, and authority in the family, as in government, resided exclusively with men.

Justine

The original version of *Justine*, entitled *Les Infortunes de la vertu* (*The Misfortunes of Virtue*), was not so much a novel as a short story with satirical aims. It was composed in 15 days, in the Bastille in 1787. Largely conventional in style, and completely lacking in obscenity, this well-written and fast-moving novella contains an intensity and clarity of vision absent from the two subsequent versions, but it was destined never to reach the reading public in the author's lifetime. The unpublished *conte* was, nevertheless, to grow into the novel-length *Justine ou Les Malheurs de la Vertu (Justine, or The Misfortunes of Virtue)*, which appeared anonymously in 1791, a year after the author's release from Charenton. Sade claimed that his editor had pressured him to write a 'spicy' bestseller. The editor must have been delighted with the result. *Les Malheurs* was considerably more violent and sexually explicit than *Les Infortunes*, and sold so well that five further editions had to be printed in the space of ten years. While the public's appetite for Sade's first published work was evidently insatiable, critical responses of the time were mixed. An article of 27 September 1792 praises the author's 'rich and brilliant' imagination, while exhorting young people to 'avoid this dangerous book' and advising 'more mature' men to read it 'in order to see to what insanities human imagination can lead', but then to 'throw it in the fire'. In a letter to his lawyer, Reinaud, Sade himself conceded the immorality of his new novel:

> They are now printing a novel of mine, but one too immoral to send to a man as pious and as decent as you. I needed money, my publisher asked me for something quite spicy, and I made him [a book] capable of corrupting the devil. They are calling it *Justine ou les malheurs de la vertu*. Burn it and do not read it if by chance it falls into your hands: I renounce it.

In spite of the popular success of *Les Malheurs*, Sade's financial affairs remained in the doldrums. *Justine* did not make its author any money, nor did any of his other books. It did, however, achieve a *succès de scandale*. This apparent success and the writer's continued impecuniousness doubtless provided sufficient incentive for the composition of the much extended and more openly obscene final version of Justine's adventures, entitled *The New Justine*, which appeared eight years later, in 1799. Sade's most violent and most shocking completed work, the marathon picaresque novel, *The Story of Juliette*, was published shortly afterwards, some time between 1799 and 1801. It was the last straw for the Paris Prefect of Police, Dubois, who was already determined to hunt down the author of *Justine*. Dubois was convinced that both were the work of the same man. Eventually, probably acting on a tipoff from one of the many police informers who haunted the Parisian book-trade, police officers of the new and highly censorious Napoleonic régime arrested Sade and his publisher, Nicolas Massé, at Massé's offices on 6 March 1801. Sade was allegedly caught with the manuscript of *Juliette* in his hand. Copies of both works were seized, and Sade was charged with having written what has been considered to be the most depraved novel of all time. He was immediately imprisoned, and would remain incarcerated until his death in 1814.

In a sense, then, Sade fell victim to his own creation. Perhaps all along, as his narrative became increasingly more bold and more challenging to the censor, the author was unconsciously driven to a point of coincidence with his fictional heroine, for both author and character are acutely aware of their own status as victim. After all, it was not Juliette but Justine that preoccupied him for more than ten years of his own less than happy existence, to the point of composing three separate versions of her woeful tale. Such, in fact, was the association of Sade with his less fortunate heroine that he would be known throughout the 19th century as the author, not of *Juliette*, but of *Justine*. This identification of the writer with his ingenuous creation outside of the text can perhaps be explained by what some have seen as an unconscious authorial identification on psychological and emotional levels with the character herself, to the point of sympathizing masochistically with her suffering. We shall return to this hypothesis.

From the outset, Justine appears to us as a passive creature, destined for martyrdom. A devout young girl of 12 at the beginning of her remarkable odyssey, her religious faith remains implausibly unshaken by the unending catalogue of disasters that befall her throughout her relatively short and miserable existence. Sade deftly sketches the charm of this 'delicious' young creature in terms of what we in the West would now consider to be a stereotype of feminine beauty (big blue eyes, teeth of ivory, lovely blonde hair). For the modern reader, the same physical features make up another stereotype – the dumb blonde – which is reinforced here by character traits connoting 'girlishness' and vulnerability (ingenuousness, sensitivity, generosity of spirit). Like her beauty, these traits can be also read at the very surface of her body: modesty, delicacy, shyness, and, above all, the 'look of a virgin'. In fact, in line with her creator's materialist thinking, physique and temperament become one in Justine: naivety is graceful, vulnerability attractive, sexual innocence seductive. Justine is the first 'girly girl', the young ingénue so beloved of 19th- and 20th-century theatre and film, a blonde whose dumbness here means ignorance of sexuality, an essential prerequisite of female victimhood in Sade's fictional universe. Justine's physical appearance immediately suggests that this is the part she will play: in Sade's terms, she is primed to be a victim of her own virtue – which will prevent her from enjoying the sexual attentions forced upon her, but which, more importantly, will determine the very nature of her attraction for the men and women who abuse her. She will also be the victim of the religious and social prejudices of a society that places a high value on the status of virginity, and in so doing creates a taboo that cries out to be transgressed. Innocence, virtue, beauty are all synonymous in Justine, who, initially at least, is nothing more than a cluster of nouns and adjectives. She is simply, we are told, the embodiment of virginal innocence and sensibility, having a potentially erotic vulnerability, 'an ingenuousness, a candor that were to cause her to tumble into not a few pitfalls' (*Good Conduct*, p. 459). A construct of Platonic ideals expressed unplatonically in physical terms, Justine exists in abstraction only, as an object promised to the reader's sexual curiosity – until the narrative brings her to life, that is.

In all of these respects, Juliette is an exact opposite and, like her sister Justine, her character and temperament are initially expressed in physical terms: not blonde, but brunette, with eyes not credulously blue but dark and 'prodigiously expressive'; not timid but spirited; not naive but incredulous; not innocent but worldly wise, thanks to the best possible education that a father's untimely ruin will deny her younger sister.

When both parents die and the two girls are left penniless orphans, Juliette's only response is the pleasure of being free. Even if we had not already been told at the beginning of the narrative of the fortune her beauty will help her to amass, we would know from this display of lack of feeling that, far from being a victim, the insensitive and self-serving Juliette will be one of life's winners. Not so the 'sad and miserable Justine'.

Justine's narrative follows more or less the same pattern in all three

The three *Justine*s

(1) *Les Infortunes de la vertu* (1787). Translated as *The Misfortunes of Virtue*. Referred to here as *Les Infortunes*.

(2) *Justine, ou les Malheurs de la vertu* (1791). Translated as *Justine, or the Misfortunes of Virtue*, or as *Good Conduct Well Chastised*. Referred to here as *Les Malheurs* (French edition) and *Good Conduct* (English edition).

(3) *La Nouvelle Justine* (1799). Translated as *The New Justine*. Referred to here as *The New Justine*.

versions, although, in the second and especially the third versions, events are narrated in considerably more detail. As the subtitle of the first published version implies, the virtuous heroine's progress through the novel is one of unrelenting misfortune.

Although Justine tries to do the right thing in every dilemma that befalls her, the consequences of her actions are always greater misery. Her naivety cynically exploited by every man she meets, including one whose life she has saved, she is systematically raped, branded as a criminal, held captive in a monastery by lubricious and murderous monks, savaged by dogs, her blood drained by a vampiric Bluebeard figure, subjected to any number of perverse practices, framed for a crime she did not commit, and, eventually, condemned to the gallows by a corrupt judge. Pausing with her guards at a staging-inn on her way to be hanged, Justine encounters her sister Juliette, travelling under the name of Madame de Lorsange, and recounts her story to her, and indirectly, therefore, to the reader. In the first two versions, when she finishes her sad tale, Justine is recognized by Juliette as her long-lost sister, Juliette's rich and powerful lover succeeds in rescuing her from the gallows, and she goes to live with them in their château. Fate, however, cruelly

15. André Masson, drawing for *Justine*, 1928

cuts short Justine's life and her new-found happiness. In a savage metaphor for the sheer perversity of providence, she is finally split asunder by a thunderbolt during a violent storm. The evolution of this scene and its repercussions in the narrative reflect both the increasingly transgressive sexualization of *Justine* from one version to the next and, perhaps also, the author's changing attitude to his heroine. In *Les Infortunes*, the bolt enters her right breast and comes out through her mouth, whereas in *Les Malheurs*, the bolt exits through her abdomen, and in *The New Justine* through her vagina. Furthermore, in the final version, in which there is no happy reunion, Justine's horrific death is not so much an accident as an event engineered by Juliette and her libertine friends, who sadistically drive her outside as the storm reaches its peak.

The common theme of all three narratives is that the heroine's unreasonable attachment to virtue (and, in particular, to her virginity) attracts nothing but misfortune, as she is exploited and abused physically and sexually by almost everyone she encounters, and is even framed for crimes of theft and murder.

Justine may be read as a satire, attacking the corruption of contemporary institutions, including the judiciary, banking, the bourgeois-dominated world of finances in general, and above all the Catholic Church, with divine providence the principal religious target. Sade's libertines dismiss belief in a deity altogether, and draw the logical conclusion from the observation that the virtuous perish while the wicked survive, insisting that 'in an entirely corrupted age, the safest course is to follow along after the others' (*Good Conduct*, p. 457). Rousseau's idealistic faith in Man's natural goodness is directly challenged in a dissertation delivered to Justine by Roland the counterfeitor: the only truth is the law of nature, according to which the strong not only survive but flourish at the expense of the weak. In the original version, even Justine herself comes to the conclusion on encountering the monstrous counterfeitor that 'Man is naturally wicked'.

The use of models such as the fairy tale, the Gothic novel, and the moral tale, drawn from the popular literature of the time, has a clear impact on the verisimilitude of the narrative. Whatever her injuries, Justine always makes a perfect and speedy recovery, often thanks to quasi-magical healing potions: 'He picks up a flask of spirits and several times rubs all my wounds. The traces of my executioners' atrocities vanish' (*Good Conduct*, p. 733); and even the mark of the thief branded on her shoulder is completely removed by surgeons following her reunion with Juliette. Like the hero or heroine of some modern comic-book adventure story, she extricates herself with astounding ease from all the mortal perils that beset her. The bloodthirsty Gernande, for example, forgets to lock the door of her prison, and with one bound she is free! At the level of characterization, too, there is little concern with plausibility. That the common thieves, la Dubois and Coeur-de-Fer, should discourse like philosophers is unlikely, to say the least. We should, of course, not be surprised by this lack of attention to verisimilitude. Sade's fiction is a long distance from the realism that will come to dominate, and in many ways define, the novel genre in the 19th century. As a writer of the 18th century, Sade is simply of his time.

The third and final version of the tale *The New Justine* is considerably longer – there are many new scenes and characters – and far more violent than the preceding versions. *The New Justine* and *The Story of Juliette, her Sister*, which were published as a single work, together fill ten volumes and nearly 3,700 pages, 'adorned with a frontispiece and one hundred carefully wrought engravings'. All of these illustrations depict lewd scenes, including naked men, women, children, and sometimes animals engaging in orgiastic activity, in which flagellation and sodomy are dominant. The male organs are always erect and sometimes in the process of ejaculating. Most of the female figures are in the posture of passive and pleading victims. In *The New Justine* alone, there are 40 such illustrations. According to a contemporary newspaper article, these covered one-third of the pages of the novel. Though something

16. Engraving for the first illustrated edition of *La nouvelle Justine, suivi de l'Histoire de Juliette, sa soeur.* Printed in Holland, 1797

of an exaggeration, this inflated perception of the number of engravings does nevertheless convey the impact of these volumes on the public of the time. Jean-Jacques Pauvert observes that this was no less than 'the greatest undertaking of print pornography ever accomplished'.

In addition to being much longer, the final version of *Justine* differs radically from the two previous versions with regard to moral intent. There is in *Les Infortunes* and *Les Malheurs* a transparently hypocritical attempt to construct a moral lesson. In a factitious and highly ironic 'happy ending', Juliette and her lover are sufficiently moved by her sister's sudden death to follow the path of virtue to true happiness. Juliette joins a Carmelite convent and becomes the very embodiment of piety, whilst her lover embarks on a successful and exemplary career in government. On the basis of events that directly contradict the lessons in self-interest of the entire preceding narrative, the reader is invited to draw the wholly implausible conclusion that

> true happiness is to be found nowhere but in Virtue's womb, and that if, in keeping with designs it is not for us to fathom, God permits that it be persecuted on Earth, it is so that Virtue may be compensated by Heaven's most dazzling rewards.
>
> (*Good Conduct*, p. 743)

This conclusion is unconscious hypocrisy at best and a purely pragmatic measure to avoid censorship at worst. In stark contrast, the ending of *The New Justine* shows that Sade has abandoned all former pretences at writing a morally uplifting tale. Neither Juliette nor any of her companions undergoes a Pauline conversion to virtue – quite the opposite in fact – and the reader of *Juliette* is left in no doubt as to the rewards of vice.

The first and second versions also possess a common narrative structure, which *The New Justine* does not share. With the exception of the briefest of introductions and conclusions, narrated in the third person by an authorial voice, both *Les Infortunes* and *Les Malheurs* are first-person narratives, offering direct access to the heroine's thoughts and feelings and permitting the development of an unmediated relationship between character and reader, whereas the exclusively third-person narration of the final version creates an affective distance between them. An authorial voice dominates *The New Justine*, directly controlling the reader's responses, telling him what to think of a heroine whose speech is confined within quotation marks and at every turn qualified by an author-narrator's accompanying commentary. These differences of narrative voice have an impact on style. Whereas the third-person narrator of *The New Justine* is free to describe sexual activities in a manner that is direct to the point of obscenity, earlier versions are narrated by Justine herself, whose modesty naturally forbids any use of obscene language to describe what happens to her, giving rise to a largely euphemistic and, arguably, more inventive style.

All versions of *Justine* contain elements of black comedy, but the authorial narrative of the final version makes for a less subtle brand of humour than the first-person narratives of *Les Infortunes* and *Les Malheurs*. In *The New Justine*, the humour is more visual than verbal, recalling the knockabout sexual farces of Chaucer or Boccaccio. Much of it is simply coarse and puerile, focusing frequently on the size and power of libertine organs: Coeur-de-Fer's erect penis is hard enough to break open a walnut, while the monk Severino's member 'protruded above the table by six inches'. The embedded narrative of Jérôme's first sexual experiences with his sister is full of comic mishaps and misapprehensions.

The constraints associated with *Les Infortunes* and *Les Malheurs*, especially the first-person narration, also tend to make us sympathize more with the narrating heroine. Indeed, as was suggested above, Sade may have been drawn to identify masochistically with his creation. It is certainly undeniable that the two have a great deal in common. Like Justine, Sade suffered much the same reversals of fortune: loss of wealth and property in the Revolution; being branded a criminal (symbolically in his case); what he saw as the abuses of justice in the magistrates' courts; the threat of the death penalty; and, not least, the tortures of a captivity whose term was unknown to him.

This view finds some support in the portrayal of Justine herself. Notwithstanding her initial portrait as the brainless and bashful blonde with an unreasonable and unthinking devotion to virtue, Justine actually behaves in an entirely sensible and sympathetic manner. In spite of himself, perhaps, Sade creates a figure with whom it is not hard to sympathize. The entire story is, after all, centred around Justine, and so she is the focus both of the libertines' attention within the text and of the reader's attention outside it. Justine herself expresses an ironic awareness of the central role that her status as victim gives her: 'I am the focal point of these execrable orgies, their absolute center and mainspring' (*Good Conduct*, p. 733). The centrality of her role as victim is complemented and, indeed, enhanced by the centrality of her role as narrator. Because it is Justine and not the author-narrator who has charge of the narrative in *Les Infortunes* and *Les Malheurs*, she is able to condemn the libertines for their views and is even accorded the right to put her own case at length, for instance, on the question of God's existence. Since she is the principal narrator, both libertines and fellow victims speak through her, which means that we mostly share a point of view that is opposed to, and sometimes mocking of, that of the libertines.

Contrary to the impressions given by her initial character-sketch, she is intelligent and self-assertive in debates with her libertine captors, who always listen respectfully to her arguments and at times even compliment her reasoning.

Far from being the naive ingénue, Justine, even in her final incarnation, is actually a smart, resilient young woman whose concern for others leads her repeatedly into danger. Her most horrendous experiences befall her not because of her naivety, but because of the wickedness of Man. It is not Justine's virtue that makes life difficult for her – she finds ways of justifying to herself her acquiescence in the various sexual acts demanded of her – but the moral dilemmas that so frequently confront her. In these situations, which involve the choice between two evils, Justine shows herself to be thoroughly pragmatic. One of the best examples of such 'double-binds' is the episode at d'Esterval's 'cut-throat' inn in *The New Justine*, where travellers are routinely robbed and murdered. D'Esterval challenges Justine to help the victims to escape; if she succeeds, she too will be set free, but if she fails, she will remain to witness the deaths of more unfortunates. Were she to run away and denounce him to the authorities, more would have died before they could take action. This is the kind of moral dilemma that the German philosopher, Immanuel Kant, had written about only a decade earlier in his *Critique of Practical Reason* (1788), a work that may well have influenced Sade. Indeed, in this work, Kant describes an almost identical situation to that confronting Justine, whereby a man saves others in a shipwreck, but in the process loses his own life. For Kant, exemplary acts are often fraught with moral contradictions, and there can be no clear guidelines to determine the most moral course of action, since moral purpose is entirely absent from the faculty of reason. Justine frequently finds herself on the horns of similar dilemmas and responds to them with a Kantian pragmatism, assessing how to achieve the best outcome for all concerned in the circumstances. In thus demonstrating the uselessness of searching for moral resolutions to practical problems, Sade embraces a Kantian perspective that is, in this respect at least, in tune with his own rejection of moral absolutes.

Whatever Justine does, however, invariably leads to more dilemmas and more misfortune. In fact, Sade's novel is not so much an attack on the foolishness of virtue as on notions of Man's natural goodness and of a benevolent providence. Fate does exist, but it is evil, not good. Sade's universe is consequently as Manichaean as it is materialist, and the responsibility of individuals like Justine for the plights in which they find themselves is diminished as a result. (The gloomy philosophy of Manichaeanism posits two equal forces of good and evil in the universe, a tension that explains the frequent prevalence of moral and physical evil. There is no evidence of a divine providence, since Nature appears devoid of any moral sense.)

The Story of Juliette

Like *Justine*, the thousand-page-long *Story of Juliette* may be read as a savage attack on the corruption of 18th-century French society, in which money is power, and power facilitates the unrestrained pursuit of pleasure. More so than *Justine*, however, *Juliette* also represents the expression of a desire for such unfettered freedom – a Utopic vision of power that is almost divine in its totality. Only the leisured upper classes could afford to use sex recreationally as well as procreationally, and only the political masters of a land could indulge with impunity in a perverse sexuality that privileged rape and murder, manipulating the justice system for their own ends. Once again, Sade chooses a woman as the focus of the narrative, but Juliette is no victim, any more than the violent and depraved *femmes fatales* who befriend her.

Sade's longest novel is scandalously provocative with regard to the role and status of women, as well as to a whole range of moral and philosophical issues, and there is no doubt that many will continue to find both the ideas contained within its pages and its outright obscenity unpalatable. On the other hand, it is a work of breathtaking geographical and historical scope and of remarkable scholarship, replete with learned allusions and references and detailed philosophical arguments. But at the simple story level, too, the novel's sheer nervous energy carries the reader along with its heroine as she travels through a Europe ruled by sexual deviants and ruthless megalomaniacs. Among its hundreds of characters, we encounter lascivious monarchs and psychotic politicians, atheistic clerics and man-hating lesbians, giants and sorcerers, vamps and virgins. The entirely fictional rub shoulders with the verifiably historical; the real blends with the surreal (a black mass at the Vatican, the giant Minski's 'human' furniture) to produce a work of layered complexity. Sade's *Juliette* can be read on many levels: as an adult fairy tale and a manual of sexology; as a political and philosophical satire and the most gruesome of horror stories; as a European travelogue and an 18th-century 'road movie'; above all, perhaps, as a terrifying journey into the murkier depths of human eroticism. On all of these levels, *Juliette* goes much further than *Justine*. The narrative moves faster, the crimes are greater, and the reader feels swept along from one location to another to encounter ever more extreme situations and behaviour.

Juliette, we remember, is Justine's beautiful but ruthless elder sister, and her opposite in every way. She has, in fact, much in common with Eugénie, the mother-hating apprentice libertine of *Philosophy in the Boudoir*. Fifteen years old when she and Justine are orphaned, she is Eugénie let out of the boudoir into the wide and wicked world. Already awakened to the pleasures of the body, as well as to its power, by the mother superior of the convent where the two sisters had resided before their father's financial ruin, she immediately sets out to make her living as a prostitute, becoming the mistress of two extremely dangerous libertines, Noirceuil and Saint-Fond. The latter is a government minister who abuses his position to line his pockets and to evade the consequences of the rapes and lustmurders that he and his associates regularly commit. Under the protection of these two monsters, she embarks with her lesbian lover, the equally bloodthirsty Clairwil, on an epic tour of Europe and especially Italy, encountering *en route* a series of libertines, each more depraved than the last, and leaving a trail of pillage, death, and destruction in her wake. These libertines include a number of historical figures, such as Catherine the Great, the atheistic Pope Pius VI, and two homicidal siblings of Marie-Antoinette's, Grand Duke Leopold of Tuscany and the wife of the King of Naples. Unsurprisingly, given the revolutionary period in which the novel was written, kings and pontifs are seen as surpassing all others in their debauchery and corruption. Eventually, following many horrendous and often gratuitous crimes, which include the murder of her friend Clairwil, Juliette returns considerably enriched to France. There she is reunited with Noirceuil, whose iniquities are seen to be rewarded when the King makes him prime minister, assuring him and his fellow criminals of a glorious future. With a note of self-referential irony, Noirceuil draws the obvious moral from their story:

> Come, good friends, let us all rejoice together, from all this I see nothing but happiness accruing to all save only virtue – but we would perhaps not dare say so were it a novel we were writing.
>
> (p. 1193)

In continuing ironic vein, Juliette adopts and defends the real author's point of view:

> Why dread publishing it, said Juliette, when the truth itself, and the truth alone, lays bare the secrets of Nature, however mankind may tremble before those revelations. Philosophy must never shrink from speaking out.
>
> (p. 1193)

So the novel ends with Juliette stepping out of the pages of her own story to take a cheeky swipe at the censor, who is implicitly positioned as the enemy of truth.

Robbing the deeply moral Justine of narrative authority in *The New Justine*, Sade then hands it over to her amoral sister in *Juliette*. With the exception of the last few pages, the entire text consists of Juliette's first-person narration of the events of her life to her sister Justine, and two male friends, a marquis and a chevalier. Now, on the face of it, such a narrative structure would seem to privilege a feminine perspective, as in the first two versions of *Justine*, although this time the female narrator would not be a victim, but a member of the libertine master class. As such, while she certainly becomes the sexual object of more or less all the men she meets, Juliette is at the same time an active and self-determining subject, proving herself to be just as calculating, just as immoral, and just as cruel as any of the male libertines who surround her. *Juliette* teems with male libertines, but most of them merge in the memory. Even Juliette's leading men, Saint-Fond and Noirceuil, perform a double act that makes them at times indistinguishable as symbols of evil and political corruption. On the other hand, here at last, or so it seems, is the portrayal in fiction of an intellectually strong and sexually liberated woman, a female model that the surrealist poet Guillaume Apollinaire found sufficiently positive to describe as the woman of the future, this 'creature that we cannot yet conceive, but which is freeing itself from humanity, which will take wing and will renew the universe'.

Juliette also contains a number of other strong female characters. There is the witch and poisoner, Durand, and the lesbian Clairwil, who sees it as her duty to avenge the victims of her sex by murdering as many men as possible. Transparently as part of a wider campaign of rehabilitation of the *divin marquis*, some have made much of this theme of female liberation running along the surface of Sade's novel. According to this perspective, the creator of the omnipotent Juliette was nothing less than a precursor of modern feminism. Sadly, however, this impression is only superficial, for in every important respect, both Juliette and her girlfriends are quite simply male surrogates.

If Sade wants women to be sexually free, it is, in the end, because he wants them to be sexually available. Moreover, his conception of an active female libido is fundamentally male-centred.

In *Boudoir*, as throughout the Sadean *oeuvre*, attitudes to women are ambivalent at best, self-contradictory at worst.

Even at the level of narrative structure, the ostensibly feminine authority of Juliette as narrator is seriously undermined by a complexity of form that privileges numerous male voices. In a variety of ways, the third-person authorial narrative, which is of course male in perspective, frames and controls Juliette's own: outside of Juliette's narration of her story to Justine, the marquis and the chevalier, is the author-narrator, who from time to time interrupts Juliette and finally reasserts himself in the novel's closing pages to describe to the reader directly the eventual fate of his protagonists – Justine's death in the thunderstorm, the elevation of Noirceuil, the survival of Durand, and the continuing prosperity of Juliette – and to draw the morals of his story. But the male authorial presence also makes itself felt in other, more subtle ways. Numerous intertextual allusions, for example, to contemporary philosophers such as Diderot, Montesquieu, Rousseau, d'Holbach, and La Mettrie, as well as to classical writers like Molière and Machiavelli, remind the reader of Sade's erudition and help to ram home his underlying philosophical message. This is also the effect of the numerous authorial footnotes and of the many extended dissertations delivered by his libertines. These disquisitions on philosophical, religious, and political matters are often founded on a dubious logic and their perspective is exclusively male. And of course, the implied male reader's sexual interests are efficiently represented outside Juliette's narrative by the marquis and the chevalier, who listen to her tale of violent debauchery with prurient eagerness. In addition to the male voice of the author himself, there are also a couple of lengthy male micro-narratives embedded within Juliette's story: Saint-Fond's tale and, especially, the hundred-page-long story of Brisa Testa, otherwise known as Borchamps. This narrative embedding sometimes extends to a second level, as, for example, with Princess Sophie's story, told by the Princess within Borchamps' own. The effect for the reader is rather like opening Russian dolls to find smaller versions inside, as narratives are found within narratives within narratives within narratives. As well as detracting from Juliette's apparent control of the narrative, this complexity of narrative form might be considered one of the novel's more innovative features.

Juliette herself is essentially a projection of her creator's male psyche. Anatomically female, Juliette nevertheless masculinizes herself both physically and mentally. Though physically possessing all the usual Sadean attributes of feminine beauty, her reproductive potential is underplayed. There is a single reference, for example, to her menstrual periods, and although she does give birth to a daughter, Marianne, we are given no details whatever of this event. Moreover, she is completely bereft of any maternal instincts, easily consenting to the horrific murder of her daughter by Noirceuil, which she herself aids and abets. In the many sexual orgies in which she participates, she is wont to strap on artificial phalluses in the form of dildos, which she actively employs to penetrate both men and other women, although, being the phallic woman she is, she naturally prefers female victims: 'I only like doing to my own sex what this whore wants to do to men' she declares, distinguishing the female targets of her sexual aggression from the male targets of Clairwil's. In fact, Juliette shares all the behavioural traits and sexual preferences of her male sodomist associates, to the extent that only the lack of the appropriate anatomical equipment prevents her from conforming exactly to that model. If her active sexual performances are intrinsically masculine, so too is her status as passive sexual object. Again, sodomy is the order of the day:

> They devour me, but in the Italian style: my ass becomes the unique object of their caresses [. . .] they [. . .] behave for all the world as if they are unaware I am a woman.

> (p. 738)

In a more general sense, Juliette displays attitudes and characteristics more recognizably male than female: promiscuous, goal-orientated, and prioritizing reason over emotion, she is 'l'impossible Monsieur Juliette', a woman conceived in terms of male fantasies and objectives. Her first crime, a street robbery, is committed wearing men's clothes. This is a symbolic and defining moment in Juliette's progress in libertine crime. After that, she is quickly assimilated into the male libertine world, not as the stereotypical female victim – Noirceuil excepts her from that category because of her male spirit and character – but as a sort of honorary male. She is accepted without difficulty into the male libertine club, The Society of the Friends of Crime, and commits as many lustmurders as any of the men around her.

In every significant aspect of her behaviour, then, Juliette is no different from her male libertine companions. Anatomically, however, she remains female. This is not the case with other female libertines encountered by her. The beautiful nun Volmar has a mini-phallus, a clitoris three inches long, while Durand's vagina is 'obstructed', her clitoris 'as long as a finger', and she discharges 'like a man'. Both seem able to sodomize women with their clitoris alone: 'I was buggered as solidly as if I had been dealing with a man', declares Juliette ecstatically, as she relates her first sexual experiences with Durand, 'and from it experienced the same pleasure' (p. 1033). Defying nature and reality in every way, Sade's female sex criminals are the product of male fantasy. This fantasy is on one level a self-protection against castration anxiety, as what Freud calls the 'woman's real small penis', the enormous clitoris of these *femmes fatales* reassuringly restores the lost phallus to the female body.

On another, more erotic level, Volmar and Durand represent the impossible but ideal fusion of the masculine and the feminine that Sade unconsciously craves, creatures of the phallic-anal eroticism that defines his sexual universe. Many of the libertines turn away from breasts, and especially the vagina, in disgust, preferring to conceive of feminine beauty as purely anal. As he sodomizes a female victim, Noirceuil thinks of turning fantasy into reality by cutting away the flesh that separates the vagina from the anal canal and so literally abolishing the former while leaving the latter intact. Like the anus, the phallus is both literally and symbolically dominant in *Juliette*. All the male libertines are endowed with members of astonishing size, but the phallus's significance is also quasi-religious in nature. For the sorcerer, Durand, the phallus is nothing less than God himself. Indeed, the megalomaniac Noirceuil commands Juliette to adore his erect penis, 'worship it, this despotic engine' (p. 184), a sentiment echoed by many other libertines. Moberti, for instance, would like the entire universe to cease to exist when he gets hard. Juliette sums up the main message of the novel, and perhaps of all Sade's writing, when she observes how dangerous men are when their penises are erect.

The phallus, then, is deified as substitute for the non-existent God, but it is also the focus of a challenge to Nature that some, like Rousseau, have sought to put in God's place. Like the female libertines of the novel, Mother Nature is phallic-woman, and attitudes towards her are as complex as to women themselves: an awesome force to be worshipped, and yet, at the same time, the image of maternal indifference to be vilified and annihilated. In *Juliette*, there are two powerful images of Nature as a destructive force: the thunderbolt and the volcano. In their linearity and projective violence, both are also comparable to the phallus.

The thunderbolt-phallus that strikes Justine dead, in the final version of this scene in *Juliette*, enters her body through her mouth and exits through her vagina. So Phallic Nature restages the loss of Justine's virginity from above, as it were, and at Phallic Man's bidding (at Noirceuil's suggestion, the hapless Justine is exposed to the effects of a violent storm as a way of tempting Providence). The novel ends with an event that can be read symbolically as a successful attempt to control Nature.

The volcano is a clearer symbol than the thunderbolt of the ambivalence of the libertine relation to Nature: fascination and admiration, on the one hand, and envy and hatred on the other. The volcano represents the evil side of Mother Nature, which is its true face, that of a cruel stepmother, indifferent to her children. A universe without laws (which for Sade is synonymous with the indifference of Nature), would have the phallic explosiveness of the volcano: 'without laws the world turns into one great volcano belching forth an uninterrupted spew of execrable crimes' (p. 732). Like the thunderbolt, the volcano represents a challenge to libertine power: if the libertine can control its energies, then he has bested Nature. The pupil will then have defeated the master, since Nature is the model for all he does. As sources of phallic violence, libertine and volcano are in fact mirror images of each other. The ejaculations of the libertines are evoked as volcanic phenomena: they are 'eruptive discharges', threatening those around them. Sometimes they are directly compared to volcanic erruptions – of Moberti, for example:

> His discharge had been awesome, more like a volcanic eruption than anything else; his comportment was that of a wild animal than that of a human being.
>
> (p. 1097)

Juliette's imagination is fired by the volcanicity of Italy, which becomes its metaphorical expression. Two volcanoes frame Juliette's progress through Italy – Pietra-Mala in the north and Vesuvius in the south – and can be read as the symbolic expression of her growing sexual, political, and intellectual force.

The phallus, then, is at the very centre of *Juliette*'s sexual universe, not only as an essential referent, but as an all-pervasive and deeply signifying image. As for the sexual activities depicted in the novel, they all are essentially masculine in nature.

Even the tribadism (or lesbianism) engaged in by Juliette with her female friends is represented in the text from a voyeuristically male perspective, as the heterosexual male reader is implicitly invited to identify with Juliette. This identification is facilitated by an emphasis in these scenes on phallic-style penetration by dildos and on cunnilingus, in which the tongue takes on a particularly phallic character. The Sadean orgy does appear to abolish gender boundaries to some degree, reducing participants, whether male or female, to the status of objects for penetration. However, this androgyny is only superficial, since the orgy privileges phallic dominance of the predominantly female and child victim.

Juliette contains a veritable catalogue of perverse sexual practices, most with strongly violent components, that psychoanalysis associates with male sexuality: fetishism, exhibitionism, voyeurism, sexual masochism, sexual sadism, paedophilia, zoophilia, and necrophilia abound in *Juliette*. As in *The 120 Days*, one is struck by the encyclopaedic breadth of Sade's knowledge of human sexuality, the accuracy of which is borne out in many modern studies. When Juliette and Durand set up a brothel in Venice, for instance, we are given thumbnail sketches of the perversions of different clients, closely resembling aspects of the lost work in both format and content.

Violence and transgression

Sadism, the perversion for which Sade is famous and which may be interpreted in terms of a hostility towards the female body, is central to all the sexual activities represented, and takes a variety of forms. Flagellation – mainly of women and children – is a common feature of the Sadean orgy, usually as a preliminary to more horrific forms of violence, occasionally as a slow and painful method of killing. In a lengthy dissertation on murder in *Juliette*, Braschi (Pope Pius VI) insists on the cruelty of method as essential to pleasure: 'killing is not enough, one must kill in hideous style' (p. 791). In *Juliette*, especially, the victims are subjected to increasingly horrific manifestations of sexual violence that many readers will find hard to stomach. In the novel's final orgy, for instance, Noirceuil and Juliette hold a libertine 'Last Supper', in which the two reach a climax of murderous depravity: while sodomizing one of his sons, Noirceuil has Juliette tear out his heart, which he proceeds to devour, simultaneously plunging a dagger into his other son's heart; after he has also sodomized Juliette's own daughter, Marianne, the mother helps Noirceuil burn her alive.

As for *Justine*, there is no doubt that the third version of the story, in particular, contains scenes of horrendous sexual violence. However, there are comparatively few murders in *Justine*, the real influence of which is due to the representation of a transgressive sexuality. In her seminal essay, *The Sadeian Woman*, Angela Carter rightly recognizes in Justine the ingenuous but sexually magnetic blonde, beloved of Hollywood cinema since the 1930s. Carter sees Justine as the prototype of the celluloid female victim, punished just for being a woman – a female Christ paying for the sin of Eve. But many of the film characters played by Greta Garbo or Marilyn Monroe, for example, are less victimal than the men who surround them. 'Girly girls' like Monroe are fetishized by male desire precisely because they represent an inaccessible sexual object. Physical perfection invites transgression, perhaps because we cannot believe that, in an imperfect world, it should be allowed to exist. Monroe's innocence is oddly protective, her blissful unawareness of her sexual power a constant source of male frustration. Sade certainly allows his male reader to enact the fantasy of satisfying this desire, but, except in the final version, satisfaction depends much less on the sadistic pleasures associated with violence to the female body than on the fantasy of creating circumstances in which the inaccessible is made accessible. The young heroine is throughout forced by circumstances to submit to the attentions of male libertines, but except in *The New Justine*, the focus is on the enjoyment of her body rather than on the force required to achieve it. She rarely suffers serious physical harm, and when she does do so, recovers quickly and completely from its consequences.

17. Engraving for the first illustrated edition of *l'Histoire de Juliette*.
Printed in Holland, 1797

All Sadean sex is based on the principle of transgression, and any perversion is itself, by definition, a transgressive activity, since it exceeds the bounds of 'normal' sexuality, which for Freud has procreation as its sole or primary object. Within Sade's text, the erotic charge depends crucially on the libertines' awareness that they are crossing recognized bounds of behaviour, by infringing moral laws (rape, murder), religious taboos (such as those on sodomy or blasphemy), conventional mores (which prohibit sex with the very old or the very young, for example), 'natural' or socially conditioned reflexes of repulsion (urophilia, coprophilia), gender or species boundaries (passive sodomy, transvestism, zoophilia). Typically, it is the very contrast – for instance between age and youth, between piety and blasphemy, or between beauty and ugliness – that the libertines find erotic.

Yet, transgression, the breaking of rules and crossing of boundaries, is not necessarily a violent activity. And even when pain is involved, the victim's pleasure is not always excluded. In a symbolic verbal enactment of all those erotic fantasies that turn upon the pain-pleasure nexus, the incomparably brutal Rodin, for instance, declares in a memorable line in *Justine* how much he loves to make a weeping girl orgasm. The consensual as well as non-consensual act of heterosexual and homosexual sodomy, the preference of so many of the libertines, and the monk Severino's ejaculation onto consecrated hosts, both in their different ways exemplify the true nature of transgression, which is less about violence or abuse than about the breaking of taboos, whether religious or sexual (the taboos on sodomy and virginity are particularly challenging because they combine elements of both).

Juliette, on the face of it at least, crosses gender boundaries to an extent practically unknown in the 18th century. It is less Juliette's acts that we find shocking than the fact that they are committed by a woman. And if Justine continues to inhabit and excite the sexual imagination, it is not because she is the embodiment of victimhood, but because she symbolizes the thrill of transgressing those powerful taboos that still condition our thinking about sex at the beginning of the 21st century.

Chapter 7
Apostle of freedom

Intellectual influence

In his *Last Will and Testament* of 1806, Sade expressed the wish that he be buried in an unmarked grave:

> The ditch once covered over, above it acorns shall be strewn, in order that the spot become green again, and the copse grown back thick over it, the traces of my grave may disappear from the face of the earth as I trust the memory of me shall fade out of the minds of all men save nevertheless for those few who in their goodness have loved me until the last and of whom I carry away a sweet remembrance with me to the grave.

Whatever the sincerity of this apparent desire for oblivion, it can hardly be said that posterity has complied. Although officially suppressed for the greater part of the last two centuries, Sade's works have never ceased to be read in private, and his influence on writers, artists, and thinkers throughout this period is undeniable. Even in the 19th century, when his reputation was at its lowest ebb and his books difficult to obtain, the shade of the infamous Marquis hovered insistently over all the century's major literary movements, from the Gothic excesses of Romanticism to the preoccupation with the seamier side of life informing many 19th-century Realist and Naturalist novels. Both *Justine* and *Juliette* were secretly read and

18. Sade's *Last Will and Testament*

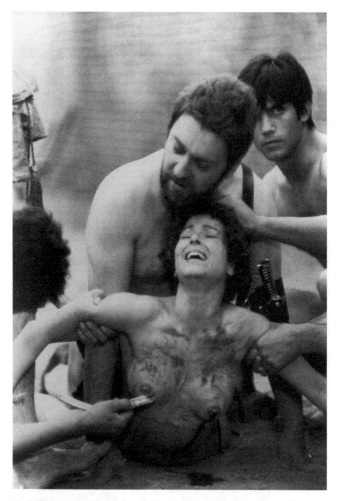

19. Still from the film *Salo or The 120 Days of Sodom*, directed by Pier Paolo Pasolini, 1975

20. Clovis Trouille, *Dolmancé et ses fantômes de la luxure* (1959)

much admired by writers on both sides of the Channel, including
Flaubert, Baudelaire, Swinburne, and many others. As early as
1843, the French critic Sainte-Beuve grudgingly conceded the
extent of Sade's influence: 'Byron and Sade [. . .] have been perhaps
the two major influences on our modern writers.' In the extra-
literary sphere, too, Sade's reputation for the depiction of violent
sexuality was already powerful enough to give rise to a new word
in the French language: *'sadisme'* first appeared in a French
dictionary (Claude Boiste's *Dictionnaire universel*) in 1834. By
the end of that century, the work of sexologists and psychoanalysts
such as Krafft-Ebing and Freud owed a considerable debt to Sade's
systematic portrayal of what came to be called 'perversions'.

It is in the 20th century, however, that Sade began to exert a more
noticeable influence on intellectual activity: from the novels of
Apollinaire, Bataille, and Robbe-Grillet in France to the films of
Buñuel and Pasolini; from Antonin Artaud's *théâtre de la cruauté*,

to the paintings of the surrealists; and, not least, in various social and intellectual movements from sexology to sexual liberation and the post-religious void. And, of course, whenever questions of pornography and censorship, or the representation of sadistic violence, are publicly debated, Sade's name is never very far away.

Critical reception

While many artists and philosophers have read Sade enthusiastically and been demonstrably inspired by him, he has not met with the same acclaim in university circles outside France. Even in France, most encyclopaedias and literary manuals largely intended for the general reader or the novice student are still reluctant to mention Sade's name, let alone devote space to any discussion of his novels, even though all of Sade's works are now freely available. Camille Paglia assesses Sade's importance and the reasons for his neglect with characteristic verve:

> The Marquis de Sade is a great writer and philosopher whose absence from university curricula illustrates the timidity and hypocrisy of the liberal humanities. No education in the western tradition is complete without Sade. He must be confronted, in all his ugliness.

In the 20th century, nevertheless, there have been occasional bursts of critical adulation, first by the surrealists in the 1920s and 1930s, later by the structuralists and the *Tel Quel* group, active from the 1960s onwards.

The rediscovery and rehabilitation of Sade in the modern era was accomplished largely by three Frenchmen: the surrealist poet Guillaume Apollinaire, for whom Sade was simply 'the freest spirit who ever lived'; Maurice Heine, who devoted the major part of his scholarly life to researching the Marquis de Sade; and Heine's spiritual heir, Gilbert Lely. It was not until the 1950s, however, that Sade's works became legally available, thanks to the courage of the

Paris publisher Jean-Jacques Pauvert, who was prosecuted for
publishing Sade in 1957.

Pauvert's eventual acquittal on appeal in 1958 led to the relaxation
of book censorship for adult readers (though not minors). After the
Pauvert trials of the late 1950s, Sade began to be more widely read,
a development that culminated in the publication of paperback
editions from the 1970s onwards. In the 1990s, Sade's writings
finally achieved the status of classical literature by being published
in the prestigious *Pléïade* series.

With the increasing availability of the work from the late 1940s
onwards came increased critical attention in France, though
Sade criticism of the late 1940s and early 1950s was certainly
not universally favourable. Both Albert Camus and Raymond
Queneau, for example, were highly critical of Sade from a political
perspective, Queneau seeing the concentration camps of Hitler and
Stalin as prefigured by his ideas.

The year 1951 saw the publication of Simone de Beauvoir's
remarkable essay 'Must We Burn Sade?', which assesses Sade as
both man and writer, combining biographical, psychoanalytical,
and existentialist approaches. This is an assessment, then, not of
Sade's misogyny, as one might have expected from the early modern
feminist, but of his evil reputation. Beauvoir warns us against
sympathizing with him too readily, because he shows little real
regard for others. He is also a second-rate writer because he writes
for himself rather than for his readers. Yet, Sade's courage in
exposing the self-interest and hypocrisy underlying man's so-called
virtues deserves our admiration and respect. Sade forces us to
recognize the truth of human nature and our potential for cruelty,
rape, and murder. Beauvoir's essay undoubtedly helped to place
Sade at the top of the intellectual agenda in France and to mount a
defence of publication in the Pauvert court case.

Beauvoir's influential essay set a trend for others to follow, and the last 50 years have witnessed a resurgence of critical interest in Sade, mainly on the part of French scholars. In the 1960s and 1970s, many leading French intellectuals such as Roland Barthes, Jacques Derrida, Michel Foucault, Jacques Lacan, Gilles Deleuze, and Philippe Sollers have published studies of Sade. Throughout recent years and into the new millennium, Sade continues to excite critical interest the world over. An Internet search in October 2004 produced no fewer than 128,000 results for 'The Marquis de Sade'. There are numerous websites, both academic and popular, dedicated entirely to Sade. The demand for biographies of Sade and critical studies of his work appears unabated, and international colloquia on Sade have been held in England (London, 1997) and the USA (Charleston, 2003).

A postmodern Sade?

Despite this variable pattern of critical reception, there is no doubting Sade's adaptability in the intellectual arena, and, consequently, his ability to survive changing intellectual fashions. As a thinker and philosopher, Sade has been recuperated by many 20th-century discourses: there has been the surrealist Sade, the Marxist Sade, the existentialist Sade, and, most surprisingly of all perhaps, the postmodern Sade.

The fundamental scepticism and rejection of all abolutes that is the basis of postmodern thinking can be traced back to the work of Friedrich Nietzsche in the 19th century, as many have observed. Few, however, have recognized the debt owed to Sade, both by Nietzsche and by postmodern philosophers. Nietzsche's doctrine of perspectivism, which claims that there are no absolute truths, only historically relative interpretations, closely resembles Sade's moral relativism. Jean-François Lyotard's argument in *The Postmodern Condition* (1979) that all of the 'grand narratives' of Western civilization, such as those of Christianity and the Enlightenment, have now been exposed as myths, certainly finds inspiration in Nietzsche's scepticism, but also in Sade's atheistic individualism and profound distrust of all collective enterprises and of the ideologies that underpin them. Sade's cynicism extended as far as the philosophical climate of optimism of the Enlightenment itself: reason, the *cri de guerre* of Voltaire, Diderot, and other 18th-century *philosophes* in their battle against religion and superstition, was itself subordinated for Sade to the anarchy of bodily desire. Sade's scandalous yet unique elevation of the body over the mind, his suspicion of reason which so often turns out to be little more than the rationalization of baser motives, finds expression in Nietzsche's emphasis on the Dionysian nature of human beings, and in Lyotard's focus on the body's libidinal drives. The poststructuralist philosopher Michel Foucault identifies an imperative to control this body in the schools, prisons, and factories of 19th- and 20th-century Europe, in service of a capitalist system that prioritizes work over leisure and packages the body itself for profit. This is a process of objectification and commodification that transforms human beings into products with as much use or exchange-value as a blow-up doll. Such an imperative is starkly prefigured in the Sadean libertines' obsessive urge to dominate their victims' bodies, to fragment them into so many sexual parts that can be abused and exchanged with others.

At the fundamental level of the construction of meaning, the Sadean text has far more in common with modernism and postmodernism than with realism. In a postmodern perspective, textual meaning is not fixed but constructed by the reader, the result of interaction between reader, text, and intertext. Sade's writing generates open circles of sexuality/textuality within which readers may discover a plurality of potential selves. These meanings flit from character to character, from situation to situation, between the authorial voice of the footnotes and dissertations, the vigorously argued responses of victimal heroines like Justine, and the ironies of a text that we are unsure should be taken seriously. Taken together, the three versions of the 'Justine' saga in a sense avoid closure by presenting us with no fewer than three different endings.

Sade's texts also repeatedly draw attention to their own textuality, which has the effect of undermining any illusion of realism. Sade's violent sexual scenarios clearly exhibit their status as writing, leaving readers distanced from a fictional world they may not wish to enter or may prefer to view as largely ludic. Such a perspective does not mean that individual readers may not identify with Sade's characters or situations on a physical level, just that such identifications will only ever take place in the minds of individual readers rather than being pre-inscribed into the text itself.

The ubiquity of dialogue in the writing is another feature that lends itself to a postmodern treatment. Dialogue is inherently pluralistic, working against the creation of a single, unified point of view. Thus, even Sade's prose works offer a multiplicity of voices, physically represented on a stage that has more in common with theatre in the round than with a conventional unified tableau framed and defined by a proscenium arch (consider the theatre at Silling with its niches and recesses, or the boudoir of Dolmancé and Saint-Ange). The manner in which at Silling story-tellers directly address their audience and spectators become actors functions to explode any reality effect, generating multiple points of view, and like medieval theatre, involving the libertine audience directly in the fictional world constructed by the story-tellers and undermining any realist illusion against which the subsequent and highly schematic sacrifice of victims might otherwise appear convincingly real.

This pluralism can be found at almost every level of the Sadean text, which mixes and confuses genres, deconstructing the opposition between comedy and tragedy (some readers will react with revulsion, others with laughter), sabotaging any attempt to identify 'positions' running through and uniting the corpus of Sade's writing. It is never possible to say, as it might be in the case, for example, of a 19th-century realist novelist such as Balzac or Stendhal, that one work illuminates the others. The very titles themselves exhibit this refusal of fixity, mixing different discourses (*Philosophy in the Boudoir* inserts the philosophical and political into the pornographic) and challenging convention with shocking inversions (*The **Misfortunes** of Virtue*, *The **Prosperities** of Vice*).

These postmodern features work against the overt attempts by an authorial voice in some texts to establish a conclusive meaning. The result is a text that ripples with inconsistencies and contradictions. Far from being a weakness, as it might be considered to be in a classic realist narrative, this characteristic plays a positive role, ensuring that Sade's writing remains open to multiple interpretations, thus preserving its accessibility to different readers and, ultimately, keeping it alive for each new generation.

In this postmodern perspective, Sade's writings cannot really be considered pornography, since in spite of their extremes of obscenity and violence, and their repeated infringement of social, moral, and religious taboos, a frequent combination of comic exaggeration with elements of irony, parody, and satire seriously undermines any erotic potential. The violence is itself too self-consciously extreme to be taken seriously. Indeed, the writing generally displays too much awareness of itself *as text* to be sexually arousing for the majority of readers. But in the end, this is an issue for each individual reader to decide. Like any fiction, Sade's stories exist only on paper and in the reader's imagination, and are no more dangerous than the mind of the person reading them. Sade created a corpus of writing of astonishing breadth and unparalleled complexity that shines a light into those dark corners of the human psyche from which most of us would prefer to avert our gaze. That he does so with skill, erudition, playfulness, and not a little humour more than entitles him to a place in the Western literary and philosophical tradition.

Sade's legacy

In the moral and political arenas, Sade's thought has never seemed more relevant than in a 21st century as marked as any previous age by a violence that is religious in origin. In caricaturing the corruption of organized religion and in exposing the absurdities of religious faith, Sade is one of the first powerful voices of a new, secular era that began in the 19th century. On the other hand, the threats currently posed both by Islamic fundamentalism (world terrorism and indiscriminate kidnapping and murder) and by evangelical Christianity (reactionary sexual politics, leading to anti-gay, anti-abortion, and anti-stem-cell research campaigns) are stark reminders of the excesses to which uncompromising idealism and belief in absolute truth can lead, excesses that Sade repeatedly warns against. In unmasking the megalomanias and perversions of barons and bankers, of monarchs and magistrates, Sade equally warns against naive trust in all forms of authority. This is a message that, in an era of spin doctors and sleaze, of multi-national monoliths and military crusades, we would do well to heed.

In his libertine writings, and in many aspects of his own behaviour, Sade is a rebel, a naughty boy put out into the corridor for not conforming to the standards of his society and, above all, for saying the unsayable, for speaking out when others keep silent. Like all rebels, Sade kicked against the traces and sometimes harmed others, most of all perhaps his own family, in the process. Yet, the rebel is a figure in history as in politics that has frequently proved essential to human progress, and Sade deserves to be viewed in this light. No other voice of the turbulent times in which Sade lived dared to expose the fundamentally sexual character of all lust for power, to link sex directly with politics and the body with philosophy. The Marquis de Sade points an unwelcome finger at emperors who appear naked on the public stage while claiming to wear new clothes, and his work remains indispensable reading for all who wish to separate reality from illusion.

Despite the undeniable contribution that Sade has made in the intellectual arena, however, his lasting impact on the world can perhaps be more readily felt in the cultural practices and sexual politics of the late 20th century, from the so-called 'permissive society' which the 'swinging sixties' ushered in, to a recognition of greater gender equality and plurality of tastes in the area of sexuality. Sade cannot, it is true, be credited as the first to advocate sex education, or sex for pleasure rather than procreation, but it is his voice above all others that we hear promoting such ideas, which are now accepted by the majority of citizens in our liberal democracies. An increasing tolerance of prostitution, pornography, consensual sado-masochistic practices, and public sexual display, acknowledgement of the principles of difference and choice, are recognizable features of contemporary Western culture, and all have a strongly Sadean resonance. Although the birth-control pill has almost certainly played the greatest role in the evolution of sexual mores from the 1960s, the general climate of sexual liberation that made its acceptance possible is more in tune with the fictions of the Marquis de Sade than with any single intellectual movement of the modern age:

> I authorize the publication and sale of all libertine books and immoral works; for I esteem them most essential to human felicity and welfare, instrumental to the progress of philosophy, indispensable to the eradication of prejudices, and in every sense conducive to the increase of human knowledge and understanding.
>
> (*Juliette*)

Further reading

Selected primary texts

Most of Sade's works have been translated into English, and the most widely available editions are listed below. With the exception of the correspondence, placed first, works are listed in approximate chronological order.

Marquis de Sade: Letters from Prison, translated by Richard Seaver (London: Harvill Press, 2000).

The One Hundred and Twenty Days of Sodom, compiled and translated by Austryn Wainhouse and Richard Seaver (London: Arrow Books, 1990).

The Misfortunes of Virtue and Other Early Tales, translated by David Coward (Oxford: Oxford University Press, 1999).

Marquis de Sade, Justine, Philosophy in the Bedroom, and Other Writings, compiled and translated by Richard Seaver and Austryn Wainhouse (New York: Grove Weidenfeld, 1990). The volume includes the second *Justine*, *Dialogue between a Priest and a Dying Man*, and *Last Will and Testament*.

The New Justine is not currently in print in English. All translations from this work are therefore my own.

Juliette, translated by Austryn Wainhouse (London: Arrow Books, 1991; translation, 1968).

The Crimes of Love, translated by Margaret Crosland (London: Chester Springs, 1996)

A slightly abridged version of 'Idée sur le roman', published under the title 'Note on the Novel', may be found in *Yale French Studies*, no. 35 (1965).

Secondary literature in English

This section lists critical works on Sade currently available in English, and is divided into two parts. Part 1 includes works for the general reader, while the more challenging studies are reserved for Part 2. A selection of biographical studies may be found in the References section (Chapter 1).

Part 1

R. Barthes, *Sade, Fourier, Loyola* (Baltimore: Johns Hopkins University Press, 1997; first published in French in 1971). One third of Barthes' original study is devoted to Sade. This is split into aphorisms that address quirky features of Sade's writing and that can be read between tube or bus stops. Brilliant and still excitingly novel.

Simone de Beauvoir, 'Must We Burn Sade?', translated by Annette Michelson (London and New York: Nevill, 1953); also in *The 120 Days of Sodom and Other Writings*, edited and translated by Austryn Wainhouse and Richard Seaver (New York: Grove Press; London: Arrow, 1990). The well-known French feminist's lengthy and lucid essay on Sade draws heavily on existentialist and psychoanalytic theory.

Angela Carter, *The Sadeian Woman: An Exercise in Cultural History* (London: Virago Press, 1979). An intelligent and inspired analysis of the feminine in Sade.

R. Darnton, *The Forbidden Best-sellers of Pre-Revolutionary France*

(London: HarperCollins, 1996). A historian's view of the pornographic genre and its influence in 18th-century France. A fascinating and well-informed study.

A. Dworkin, *Pornography: Men Possessing Women* (London: The Women's Press Ltd, 1981). Chapter 3 demonizes Sade as the quintessential woman-hating pornographer. Worth reading as one of the more intelligent examples of anti-Sade rhetoric, although Dworkin shows absolutely no sensitivity to the literary dimensions of the works.

Camille Paglia, *Sexual Personae: Art and Decadence from Nefertiti to Emily Dickinson* (New York: Vintage Books, 1991). Various passages on Sade are characteristically quirky, forthright, brilliant. Paglia's Sade is a realist who paints nature, not in the rose-tinted perspective of a Rousseau, but as she truly is, 'pagan cannibal, her dragon jaws spitting sperm and spittle'.

John Phillips, *Sade: The Libertine Novels* (London: Pluto Press, 2001). A detailed introductory study to the four libertine novels, aimed at the student and the interested general reader. Both the original French texts and the English translations of Sade's works are referenced, and quotations are given in both languages.

R. Shattuck, *Forbidden Knowledge: From Prometheus to Pornography* (New York: St Martin's Press, 1996). Chapter VII argues that Sade's works exert a pernicious influence on human behaviour. In the book's opening pages, the author warns teachers and parents that the chapter does not make appropriate reading for children and minors.

Part 2
T. Airaksinen, *The Philosophy of the Marquis de Sade* (London and New York: Routledge, 1995). A densely written study, but, exceptionally in Sade criticism, one that has the virtue of focusing solely on the philosophical thought.

D. B. Allison, M. S. Roberts, and A. S. Weiss (eds.), *Sade and the*

Narrative of Transgression (Cambridge: Cambridge University Press, 1995). This volume combines updated translations of seminal interpretations by Bataille, Lyotard, and Klossowski with essays recent enough to mention Oprah Winfrey and Hillary Clinton. It includes work by the best of recent Sade critics such as Philippe Roger, Jane Gallop, Marcel Hénaff, and Chantal Thomas. Contributions are academic, and in some cases esoteric, in approach. The most readable are those by Roger and Gallop.

Georges Bataille, *Erotism: Death and Sensuality* (San Francisco: City Lights Books, 1991). Chapters 5 and 6 are devoted to Sade, who is read in the context of Bataille's general theory of taboo and transgression. Difficult territory without a guide.

P. Cryle, *Geometry in the Boudoir: Configurations of French Erotic Narrative* (Ithaca and London: Cornell University Press, 1994). A contentious but fascinating critique of the French libertine novel with a detailed discussion of *The 120 Days*.

J. de Jean, *Literary Fortifications: Rousseau, Laclos, Sade* (Princeton, NJ: Princeton University Press: 1984). The chapter on *The 120 Days* is stimulating and highly original.

L. Frappier-Mazur, *Writing the Orgy: Power and Parody in Sade* (Philadelphia: University of Pennsylvania Press, 1996). A psychoanalytic analysis of *Juliette* that focuses on the anal-phallic nature of Sadeian sexuality. Fascinating and persuasive.

J. Gallop, *Intersections: A Reading of Sade with Bataille, Blanchot, and Klossowski* (Lincoln and London: University of Nebraska Press, 1981). Focuses mainly on the philosophical crossovers between Sade and these three modern French authors. Psychoanalytically inspired, but not narrowly so.

Marcel Hénaff, *Sade: The Invention of the Libertine Body* (Minneapolis: University of Minnesota Press, 1999). Challenging, but brilliant and original.

Pierre Klossowski, *Sade My Neighbour* (London: Quartet Books, 1992). The first to suggest that Sade's atheism is actually a case of Freudian denial; that to rail against God with such vehemence and frequency is in fact to acknowledge his existence.

Annie Le Brun, *Sade: A Sudden Abyss* (San Francisco: City Lights Books, 1991). Le Brun sets out a vigorously argued and well-researched case for viewing Sade as the first philosopher of the body in the modern era. The author is also the editor of the *Complete Works of Sade*, published in France in the 1980s by J.-J. Pauvert.

Jean Paulhan, 'The Marquis de Sade and His Accomplice', in *Marquis de Sade, Justine, Philosophy in the Bedroom, and Other Writings* (New York: Grove Weidenfeld, 1990), pp. 3–36. Argues the case that there is a psychological and emotional attachment on the author's part to Justine, and that Sade is consequently more of a masochist than a sadist.

Collected essays on Sade in English
Special edition of *Paragraph*, vol. 23, no. 1, edited by John Phillips (Edinburgh: Edinburgh University Press, March 2000).

Yale French Studies, no. 35 (1965).

The Divine Sade, PLI Warwick Journal of Philosophy (February 1994), edited by D. N. Sawhney.

Filmography
This list is restricted to films that, regardless of quality, have been directly based on Sade's life or work. Those originally made in English are asterisked.

L'Âge d'or (Luis Buñuel and Salvador Dali, 1930)

Le Vice et la Vertu (Roger Vadim, 1963)

La Voie lactée (Luis Buñuel, 1969)

De Sade (Cyril Enfield, 1971)

*Peter Weiss's *Marat-Sade* (Peter Brook, 1973)

Salo (Pier Paolo Pasolini, 1975)

Marquis (Roland Topor and Henri Xhonneux, 1988)

Quills (Philip Kaufman, 2000)

Sade (Benoit Jacquot, 2000)

References

Chapter 1

The following recent biographies of Sade together provide a detailed, readable, and balanced account of his chequered life. Of these, Bongie's offers the most critical view.

L. L. Bongie, *Sade: A Biographical Essay* (Chicago and London: The University of Chicago Press, 1998).

M. Lever, *Donatien Alphonse François, Marquis de Sade* (Paris: Librairie Artheme Fayard, 1991); translated into English as *Marquis de Sade: A Biography*, by A. Goldhammer (London: HarperCollins, 1993).

F. du Plessix-Gray, *At Home with the Marquis de Sade* (New York: Penguin Books, 1999).

N. Schaeffer, *The Marquis de Sade: A Life* (London: Hamish Hamilton Ltd, 1999).

D. Thomas, *The Marquis de Sade* (London: Allison and Busby, 1992).

Chapter 2

The Misfortunes of Virtue and Other Early Tales, translated by David Coward (Oxford: Oxford University Press, 1999). The very useful

Introduction to this edition includes a detailed discussion of the themes and motifs of Sade's short stories.

The quotation from Villeterque on p. 22 is from the *Journal des Arts, des Sciences et de la Littérature*, 22 October 1800, no. 90, pp. 281–4, and is cited by Lever, pp. 510–11.

The quotations from Sade's correspondence on pp. 24–26 are taken from du Plessix-Gray, *op. cit.*, pp. 172 and 188.

Chapter 3

On the question of Sade's alleged 'negative theology', see especially:

Maurice Blanchot, *Lautréamont et Sade* (Paris: Minuit, 1963).

Annie Le Brun, *Sade: A Sudden Abyss* (San Francisco: City Lights Books, 1991).

Jean Paulhan, 'The Marquis de Sade and His Accomplice' in *Justine, Philosophy in the Bedroom and Other Writings* (New York: Grove Weidenfeld, 1990).

Pierre Klossowski, *Sade, My Neighbour* (London: Quartet Books, 1992) and 'A Destructive Philosophy' in *Yale French Studies*, no. 35.

Chapter 4

On Sade's politics, see:

Michel Delon, 'Sade Thermidorien' in *Sade: Écrire la crise* (Paris: Belfond, 1983), pp. 99–117.

Philippe Roger, 'A Political Minimalist', in D. B. Allison, M. S. Roberts, and A. S. Weiss (eds.), *Sade and the Narrative of Transgression* (Cambridge: Cambridge University Press, 1995), pp. 76–99.

Chapter 5

On *The 120 Days of Sodom*, see Joan de Jean, *Literary Fortifications:*

Rousseau, Laclos, Sade (Princeton, NJ: Princeton University Press, 1984). On the 'needlework' scene in *Philosophy in the Boudoir*, see Angela Carter, *The Sadeian Woman: An Exercise in Cultural History* (London: Virago Press, 1979) and Marcel Hénaff, *Sade: The Invention of the Libertine Body* (Minneapolis: University of Minnesota Press, 1999).

Chapter 6

The quotation from Sade's letter to his lawyer, Reinaud, on p. 86 is taken from Lever, *op. cit.*, p. 382.

The reference to Pauvert on p. 94 is to his 'Notice Bibliographique' in *Marquis de Sade, Oeuvres Complètes*, vol. 8 (first volume of *Juliette*), p. 18.

The hypothesis of a masochistic identification by Sade with Justine was first put forward by Jean Paulhan in his essay, 'The Marquis de Sade and His Accomplice', *op. cit.*

I am indebted to Marcel Hénaff, *op. cit.*, for the description of Juliette as 'l'impossible monsieur Juliette'.

Chapter 7

The quotation from Camille Paglia on p. 116 is from her *Sexual Personae: Art and Decadence from Nefertiti to Emily Dickinson* (New York: Vintage Books, 1991), p. 235.

Index

Index

Expand your collection of
VERY SHORT INTRODUCTIONS